THE

BRITISH ESSAYISTS

WITH

PREFACES

BIOGRAPHICAL, HISTORICAL

AND CRITICAL.

BY THE

REV. LIONEL THOMAS BERGUER

LATE OF ST. MARY HALL, OXON.—FELLOW EXTRAORDINARY OF THE
ROYAL MEDICAL SOCIETY OF EDINBURGH

IN FORTY-FIVE VOLUMES

VOL. XII.

LONDON.

PRINTED FOR T. AND J. ALLMAN, PRINCES STREET,
HANOVER SQUARE.

W. Baynes and Son, Paternoster Row; A. K. Newman and Co., Leadenhall;
W. Clarke, New Bond Street; R. Saunders, Poultry; A. Panton, Strand;
R. Triphook, Old Bond Street; Wheeler and Harvill, Bristol; W. Wright,
Fleet Street; C. Smith, Strand; E. Mercer, Derby; W. Grapel and
Robinson and Sons, Liverpool; Hall and Bradley, Halifax; A. Anderson, jun. and
H. S. Baynes, jun., Edinburgh; M. Keene and C. Cumming, Dublin.

1823.

THE

BRITISH ESSAYISTS;

WITH

PREFACES

BIOGRAPHICAL, HISTORICAL,

AND CRITICAL,

BY THE

REV. LIONEL THOMAS BERGUER,

LATE OF ST. MARY HALL, OXON: FELLOW EXTRAORDINARY OF THE
ROYAL MEDICAL SOCIETY OF EDINBURGH.

IN FORTY-FIVE VOLUMES.

VOL. XLI.

LONDON:

PRINTED FOR T. AND J. ALLMAN, PRINCES STREET,

HANOVER SQUARE:

W. Baynes and Son, Paternoster Row; A. B. Dulau and Co. Soho Square;
W. Clarke, New Bond Street; R. Jennings, Poultry; J. Hearne, Strand;
R. Triphook, Old Bond Street; Westley and Parrish, Strand; W. Wright,
Fleet Street; C. Smith, Strand: H. Mozley, Derby: W. Grapel, and
Robinson and Sons, Liverpool: Bell and Bradfute, J. Anderson, jun. and
H. S. Baynes and Co. Edinburgh: M. Keene, and J. Cumming, Dublin.

1823.

Printed by J. F. Dove, St. John's Square.

TO THE
PRESIDENT AND FELLOWS
OF ST. MARY MAGDALEN COLLEGE, IN OXFORD,
ARE INSCRIBED
THE FOLLOWING PAGES
BY A MEMBER OF THEIR SOCIETY,
WHO BEING UNWILLING,
IN THE SMALLEST DEGREE,
TO INVOLVE
THE CREDIT OF SO RESPECTABLE A COMMUNITY
IN THE SUCCESS OF
HIS OWN TRIFLING UNDERTAKING,
THINKS PROPER TO DECLARE,
THAT,
WITHOUT THEIR PERMISSION,
HE HAS PRESUMED TO OFFER THEM
THIS MARK OF HIS RESPECT
AND GRATITUDE.

HE IS THEIR OBLIGED
AND OBEDIENT HUMBLE SERVANT,
THE AUTHOR.

CONTENTS TO VOL. XLI.

CONTENTS TO VOL. XLI.

BIOGRAPHICAL, HISTORICAL, AND CRITICAL

PREFACE

TO

THE OLLA PODRIDA.

OF the forty-five Essays, which compose the
OLLA PODRIDA, nine (Nos. 7, 9, 12, 13, 17,
23, 26, 29, and 33) were composed by GEORGE
HORNE, D.D. formerly president of Magdalen
College, Oxford, and afterwards bishop of Norwich. Mr. KETT, of Trinity College, Oxford,
author of the Elements of General Knowledge,
and several other works, wrote five numbers
(Nos. 4, 22, 27, 39, and 42). Number 30 was
the production of Mr. GRAVES, the author of
the Spiritual Quixote. Mr. HEADLEY, who
edited the ' Select Beauties of Antient English
Poetry,' may claim the merit of No. 16. FRANCIS
GROSE, Esq. F.A.S. contributed No. 20. No.
24 is the composition of the Rev. JOSEPH POTT,
rector of the Old Jewry; and No. 34, the production of Mr. HAMMOND, of Merton College.
Mr. BERKELY, of Magdalen Hall, Oxford,
wrote Nos. 32, 37, and 38. No. 41 was the
tribute of Mr. MAVOR. Of four letters, one
signed VIATOR, was written by the Rev. ——
AGUTTER, of Magdalen College, Oxford; and the
rest subscribed JOHN SCRIBE, JOHN CROP,

XLI.   b

and JEREMY CRAZYBONES, claim the parental
protection of Mr. LEYCESTER, of Merton College. The whole residue of the Essays, with
the exception of No. 10, of which the author is
unknown, belongs, in strict propriety of author-
ship, to Mr. MUNRO, who was the original projector of the work. Of this latter gentleman it
behoves us to say something; and we are sorry
that what we have to communicate respecting
him is only a scanty and very imperfect biographical
notice, which has no claim whatever to the name
of a life.

THOMAS MUNRO's father was the rector of
Burgate and Wortham, near Hengrave Hall in
Suffolk. The son was born in the year 1764,
and had the great advantage of receiving part
of his classical education under the auspices
of SAMUEL PARR, LL.D. who was then master of the free-school in the city of Norwich.
The good Doctor, who never forgot any of his
pupils who had the smallest ray of genius, and
who indeed contemplated all with a sort of parental solicitude for their welfare, always re-
tained, and often expressed the kindest sentiments
of regard, towards the author of the OLLA PO-
DRIDA. Had Doctor PARR been elevated to the
episcopal bench, to which he would have proved
the most able auxiliary, and the most splendid
ornament, Mr. MUNRO was to have been one of
his chaplains.

Mr. MUNRO removed from the free-school
of Norwich to St. Mary Hall, Oxford, where he
was entered a commoner. He was afterwards
elected a demy of Magdalen College. An early

marriage with a most interesting and accomplished lady made him quit the university, without waiting to attain any higher academical honours or emoluments. Lord MAYNARD presented Mr. MUNRO with the living of Easton in Essex; and here he ended his days in the year 1813.

Mr. KETT, who was his contemporary at the university, has spoken in the most handsome manner of his moral and intellectual qualities. His friends usually styled him *Tom* MUNRO; and where a man's name passes current amongst a large society of persons, by that kind of familiar abbreviation, it is generally a symptom that he is more or less an object of their affectionate regard. Mr. MUNRO's manners appear indeed to have been remarkable for an engaging suavity, mingled with much frankness of expression, and no small facility of merriment. These are characteristics that usually make a man's society much sought; that multiply the number of his acquaintance, and secure the permanent regard of his friends. He had taste without any foppery, learning without any pedantry, and piety without any parade.

Among Mr. MUNRO's auxiliaries in the production of the OLLA PODRIDA, we must not omit the mention of Bishop HORNE. His papers indeed constitute the best part of the work; but then we must consider that he wrote when his mind had been more enriched by reading, and his judgment more improved by exercise. Mr. MUNRO's essays were comparatively juvenile performances. GEORGE HORNE, afterwards bishop of Norwich, was born at Otham, near Maidstone in Kent, on the 10th of November,

1730. His father was rector of Otham. At the age of about fifteen he was elected to a Maidstone scholarship, at University College, Oxford. He took his bachelor's degree in October, 1749; and soon obtained a Kentish fellowship at the college, of which he afterwards became president.

Dr. HORNE appears, at a very early period of his academical career, to have conceived a strong liking for the Hutchinsonian philosophy, if that name may be applied to the reveries of a visionary. Not content with viewing the Mosaic dispensation as a system exclusively appropriated to the peculiar circumstances of the Jews, and to the part which they were to fill in the wise arrangements of the MORAL GOVERNMENT, Hutchinson sought, in the Mosaic writings, what they were never meant to teach;—the true philosophy of the universe. Hence he brought the writings of MOSES to argue against the principles of the Newtonian philosophy; and he sought not only for an illustration, but an evidence of the Trinity in fire, light, and spirit; which, according to him, existed in a triple union in the substance of the air. In addition to these absurdities, he endeavoured to illustrate the operations of Providence and the mysteries of nature by the medium of the Hebrew etymologies. Though Dr. HORNE did not affect to vindicate this whole mass of absurdity, yet he undertook the defence of a larger portion of it than became a sagacious critic, or a sound theologian.

Of Dr. HORNE's various works, the best, and perhaps the only one, that will be long remembered, is his Commentary on the Psalms. This work occupied him for the space of twenty years. It was begun in 1756, and not finished till 1776. Though a good deal of the doctrinal matter in the commentary will not please all classes of readers, or readers of different sects; yet there are few persons over whose hearts the religious principle has any influence, who will not be delighted with the soft, sedate, and hallowed sensibility that prevails throughout; and which almost seems, as if the commentator had discovered the art of touching that devotional lyre, with which DAVID soothed his own sorrows, or elevated the feeling of piety and strengthened the constancy of righteousness among his countrymen. The author reckoned the time, in which he prosecuted this pious work, as containing the sum of his happiest hours. Indeed, what hours can well be happier than those which are spent in similar contemplations? The feeling of THEOPATHY, as it is identified with the works of God and with the proceedings of his providence, is one of the most sublime by which the human breast can be excited, and one of the most pleasurable with which it can ever thrill.

In 1768, Dr. HORNE was elected president of Magdalen College. About the same time he married the daughter of PHILIP BURTON, Esq. of Eltham, in Kent. Three daughters were the happy fruit of this union; of whom Mary, a young lady of very attractive figure, and very interesting countenance, was long the *Belle* of the university.

Dr. HORNE was advanced to the see of Norwich in the year 1789; when he began to be prematurely sensible of decaying strength and approaching age. While he was walking with a friend towards the long flight of steps which lead

to the episcopal residence, he said with a sigh—
' I am come to these steps at a time of life, when
I can neither go up them nor down them with
safety.'

In the latter end of the year 1791, while on
his road to Bath, he experienced an attack of
paralysis, of which he died on the 17th January,
1792, in the 62d year of his age.

Few persons have been more sincere in their
religious professions, or more exemplary in their
moral habits, than Bishop HORNE. The
goodness of his heart seemed to bloom in the
hilarity of his converse, and the amenity of his
disposition.

As a preacher, Bishop HORNE excelled in
earnestness. You were convinced that his heart
was interested in the truths he expounded, and the
admonitions he gave. Hence he was usually
heard not only with profound attention, but with
a sort of glowing delight that it is difficult to
describe. His sermons resembled the affectionate
expositions of a parent, or the tender remonstrances
of a friend. His charities were extensive; and
they were the more meritorious, because there
was no parade in the performance. It would be
well for the best interests of mankind, if such
men, or none but such, always ministered in the
sanctuary.

ROBERT FELLOWES, A. M.

Oxon.

PREFACE.

A PREFACE to a work, if read at all, is generally read the first: though as generally, I believe, written the last. Few authors know the limits of their undertaking till their work is finished; but most readers begin a book with the perusal of page the first.

This custom of writing a preface when the work is complete is attended with peculiar advantages. An author having diligently pursued the thread of his labours, through a space of five hundred pages, may then certainly sit down, and inform his readers, with great deliberation, what he intends to do.

It may not be impertinent to suppose him modestly beginning in some such manner as this:

' It is my intention, in as short a compass as the nature of the subject will admit, to offer, with becoming humility, some important truths to the consideration of my readers, which will, I trust, convince them that the narrative of Captain Lemuel Gulliver abounds with gross and palpable misrepresentations, geographical mistakes, and botanical errors; and will moreover impress conviction on their minds that the whole of that too popular history is a catch-penny account, which deserves no credit. I am clearly able to prove, that such a commander as Captain Lemuel Gulliver never served in our navies; I shall also, in the course of my work, add a few observations on the nature of truth and falsehood, and conclude with a list of British commanders from the time of Admiral Drake inclusive. The whole will form a useful repository of science, be dedicated to the people of Great Britain, and is seriously recommended to the use of schools.'

Thus are we preface-writing authors justified in speaking of ourselves and our performances. Nor is it often that we rest satisfied with a protracted enumeration of our particular accomplishments; we are frequently desirous to enhance their value by asserting boldly, that all who have preceded us in similar attempts have possessed no one requisite for the proper execution of their task.

Upon the whole, however, nothing can be so proper as for an author to recommend his own work. Is not he who writes a book the most likely person in the world to know its excellences? The seeming indelicacy of becoming the herald of our own accomplishments ought not to resist the good of the community. Besides, I would ask, who scruples to commend to a purchaser his dog, his horse, or his daughter? 'They are well-bred, Sir, and well managed—This from the Godolphin-Arabian—that from Pompey of Northumberland—the other by my first wife, with a well-stocked shop in Houndsditch.'

In imitation of so laudable an example, I too shall expect not only pardon, but praise; addressing my reader in the true spirit of such modest assurance, οναιο σου ταυτης της ποικιλομαθιας—I wish you joy of this learned miscellany.

The principal intention however of this procemium yet remains unanswered. I had only in view to introduce to my readers such of my correspondents as have obliged and gratified me by their assistance; and whose permission to make my public acknowledgments to them will confer on these pages whatever credit they may appear to deserve.

By the indulgence of my valuable friend the Reverend Mr. Kett, of Trinity College, Oxford, I am allowed to inform my readers that I am indebted to him for those numbers signed Q. viz. 4, 22, 27, 39, and 42.

For number 30, I am obliged to a gentleman whose studious retirement has made him better known as the elegant author of Columella, the Spiritual Quixote, and other works of fancy and humour, than as the Reverend Mr. Graves of Claverton near Bath.

For number 16, I have to thank an intimate friend, of whose taste and abilities every one has had sufficient testimony who has fortunately seen Select Beauties of Ancient English Poetry, lately published with Remarks, by Mr. Headley of Norwich.

I am permitted to say, that for number 20, my work is indebted to Francis Grose, Esq. F. A. S.

For number 24, to the Reverend Joseph Pott, rector of the Old Jewry.

For numbers 32, 37, and 38, to Mr. Berkeley, of Magdalen-hall, Oxford.

For number 34, to Mr. Hammond, of Merton College.

For a letter, signed Viator, to the Reverend Mr. Agutter, Magdalen College.

For number 41, to the Reverend Mr. Mavor.

For three letters, signed, John Scribe, John Crop, and Jeremy Crazybones, to Mr. Leycester of Merton College.

Did I know the author of number 10, I certainly would not omit this opportunity of making him my best acknowledgments.

There is yet one other correspondent, to whom this work is indebted for those numbers which bear the signature of Z. viz. 7, 9, 12, 13, 17, 23, 26, 29, and 33.

To him I feel myself obliged, as to one who has

descended from the eminence of a superior station
to encourage an individual, whose principal merit
was, the desire of contributing to the entertainment
of others, without disgracing himself. The permission of saying from whom I have received these favours, involves an additional obligation. My motive for not using the privilege with which I am thus
indulged, is, that in announcing such a name to the
public, I might seem to have principally in view the
gratification of my vanity. I might also, perhaps, by
some awkwardness in my mode of introduction, reflect no great credit upon the person introduced.

In these pages I have occasionally taken the liberty for which I stipulated in my introductory number, and for which I have the sanction of many similar publications of more established reputation, as in
the instances of Jerry Simple, Cantwell, Polumathes,
Snub, and Socrates in Embryo, of addressing letters
to myself. If under these feigned characters I have
added to the stock of innocent amusement, or if I
may in general claim the credit of praiseworthy intentions, I am willing to believe that I may, without
any fear of the consequences, avow myself to be the
original projector and promoter of the Olla Podrida.

THOMAS MONRO, A. B.

St. Mary Magdalen College, Oxford.

OLLA PODRIDA.

No. 1—44.

Sit down and feed, and welcome to our table.
SHAKSPEARE's *As you Like it.*

"Sit down and feed, and welcome to our table."

SHAKESPEARE's *As You Like It.*

EVERY one must have observed the unpleasant situation of a bashful man, upon his introduction into a room where he is unacquainted with the company: his arms are an encumbrance to him; when addressed, he hesitates in reply, or answers with confusion; his conversation is forced, and his remarks, most likely, foreign to the purpose, and unnatural. I cannot but confess, that such is my present situation. While I am utterly unacquainted with the humours of the persons, I am addressing, my conversation must naturally be expected to turn upon the weather, the news, and the common occurrences of the day: when we are become more intimate, we shall be more communicative; we may then proceed to the discussion of various weighty points of fashion, honour, pleasure, sometimes, perhaps, descending to literature, but never to politics.

Should I unfortunately be detected in addressing complimentary letters to myself, filled with encomiums upon the elegance of my style, the purity of my language, and the versatility of my genius; I hope, with the reasonable number of my readers (and I cannot expect an unreasonable number,) it will be a sufficient excuse, that custom hath made it a necessary appendage to a work of this kind. Such

OLLA PODRIDA.

N° 1. SATURDAY, MARCH 17, 1787.

> Sit down and feed, and welcome to our table.
> SHAKSPEARE's *As You Like it.*

EVERY one must have observed the unpleasant
situation of a bashful man, upon his introduction into
a room where he is unacquainted with the company:
his arms are an encumbrance to him; when addressed, he hesitates in reply, or answers with confusion;
his conversation is forced, and his remarks, most
likely, foreign to the purpose, and unnatural. I cannot but confess, that such is my present situation.
While I am utterly unacquainted with the humours
of the persons I am addressing, my conversation
must naturally be expected to turn upon the weather,
the news, and the common occurrences of the day:
when we are become more intimate, we shall be more
communicative; we may then proceed to the discussion of various weighty points of fashion, honour,
pleasure, sometimes, perhaps, *descending* to literature, but never to politics.

Should I unfortunately be detected in addressing
complimentary letters to myself, filled with encomiums upon the elegance of my style, the purity of
my language, and the versatility of my genius; I
hope, with the reasonable number of my readers (and
I cannot expect an unreasonable number), it will be
a sufficient excuse, that custom hath made it a necessary appendage to a work of this kind. Such

letters must be written; and, if no ingenious friend will save me the trouble of transcribing them from dedications addressed to other great men, why I must even go to work myself.

Upon reviewing the different reasons which are assigned by authors for favouring the world with their publications (or, as the ungrateful world is too apt to call it, for obtruding their nonsense on the public), I find, that with some it is an alleviation of pain: with others, a diversion from melancholy contemplations: some scribble because it is cold weather, others because it is hot; some because they have nothing else to do, and others because they had better do any thing else.

To some, this *cacoethes scribendi* is a chronic complaint. I remember a man who had regularly a fit of the gout every September: he was unavoidably confined to the house, which as unavoidably produced a fit of reading, and dictating to an amanuensis (for write he could not); so that by shaking hands with him, you might discover the advance of his poem from the size and state of his chalkstones. Many of those people (who, having been long afflicted with rheumatic complaints, are become tolerable chronicles of the weather) agree in their observation, that a rainy season is apt to produce an inundation of scribblers. Thus I have known the birth of an epic poem foretold by the shooting of a corn, and an ode to Peace prophesied from a pain in the shoulder. The reason of this is obvious: wet weather confines people at home; people confined at home become sick, listless, satirical, melancholy. Now the sick man must not suffer his ideas to stagnate, the listless must have something to dissipate his *ennui*, the satirical something to vent his spleen upon, and the melancholy something to amuse him; and each, to answer his particular end—writes.

Mr. Afflatus, who ' is now a scribbler that was once a man,' caught his distemper by the merest accident in the world. He was going out a shooting, and preparatory to it employed himself in drying his powder by the fire. A spark flying out, the whole magazine was in flames; and my friend suffered so much in the explosion, from the havoc it made in the features of his face, that I scarce knew him. He was condemned for a considerable time to his chamber, and during that confinement first became acquainted with the Aonian ladies. He was driven by necessity to read; and chance having flung in his way the energetic poetry of Sir Richard Blackmore, such a *furor poeticus* was kindled in his breast, that he instantly mistook himself for a genius, and communicated his mistake to the public. I have been informed, that in his first fit of poetic frenzy, he was so considerably elevated and furious, that after having kicked down a whole set of china, the servants were obliged to be called in to hold him. The wet weather still affects him, but he is now less violent; and his domestics take no other precaution, than when they find the glass falling, or the sky clouding over, to remove every thing out of his way which might be damaged by a fall. I can now easily conceive some sly female inquiring : What, after all this detail of other people's misfortunes, can be the reason of *thy* scribbling? To which, as I am a downright kind of a being, I answer, with more truth than politeness : Because it happens to be my humour; and my dear madam, should you be half as well pleased with what you read, as I am with what I write, I shall find in you a constant reader, and you will find in me a constant attentive slave. And, since I have indulged the flattering supposition, that I may possibly find a reader or two among the ladies, I beg leave to inform them, that it is by no means my wish

to call off their attention from their work, to dismal
inquiries into the nature of truth and falsehood, to
the apophthegms of moralists, the discoveries of philosophers, or the disquisitions of the learned. I shall
frequently devote a paper entirely to their service ;
and, as I have none of those antiquated prejudices
or opinions about me, that advice may tend to the
reformation of manners ; or, indeed, that mankind
stand in any need of improvement—I shall study to
entertain them without assuming the superiority of
a dictator.

In my attempts to collect materials for this purpose, I shall hope to succeed, notwithstanding 'Oxford (according to the opinion of many) is such
a dull, insipid, out-of-the-way place, that if it were
not for the stage coaches, it would be difficult for a
body to pick up news enough in the week to furnish
a petit-maitre's pocket-book.'

There still remains a very large class of readers,
for whom I confess myself totally unable to provide.
I mean those, who (from various causes which I
shall not at present enumerate) are entertained with
nothing but anecdotes of the *beau monde*, gleaned
from waiters and unliveried gentlemen ; or the scur-
rilities of an insolent buffoon, which are unpunished
because they are unworthy of notice.

That my attention has not been engaged in pursuits which will enable me to gratify such tastes, I
do not repine.

> Cur ego laborem notus esse tam prave,
> Cum stare gratis cum silentio possim ?—MARTIAL.

' Why should I labour in vicious industry, when I
may remain without toil in innocent silence ?'

I should in vain endeavour to convey to my readers any very accurate idea of my proposed plan, as
that which is in itself incomplete must be imperfect

in description. Thus far I can venture to promise them; that, however little pleasure they may reap from perusing the produce of a gayer hour, or however little instruction from the lucubrations of a graver one, they will not have occasion to reproach me with having willingly disseminated error, having made my correspondence with the public the vehicle of private calumnies, or ministered by my pen to the gratification of vice.

I may now, perhaps, be forgiven, if I say a few words of myself; and having entered upon that favourite topic on which the dull can expatiate with brilliancy, and the sterile with copiousness, let me obtain the negative praise of not having been prolix. I shall only then add, that I am in good health, neither sick, listless, satirical, nor melancholy; and, that I shall be thankful for the communications of all correspondents, and object to the publishing of nothing which is not devoid of candour, delicacy, common sense, or grammatical correctness.

> ———pereat mea Musa, dolosum
> Si quando ornaret vitium, aut cecinisse recuset
> Virtutemque, artemque, et quicquid carmine dignum.
>
> Monro.

Nº 2. SATURDAY, MARCH 24, 1787.

Laudant illa, sed ista legunt.—Martial.

The elegant and justly-admired author of the Adventurer[*] censures the practice of our instructors of youth for making their pupils more intimately ac-

* Nº 75.

quainted with the Iliad than the Odyssey of Homer.
I fear he has done this without producing, by his
arguments, a reformation in the conduct of some,
who still persist in the prosecution of their plan; or
conviction in the minds of others, who may have
altered it.—' This absurd custom,' says he, ' which
seems to arise from the supposed superiority of the
former poem, has induced me to make some reflections on the latter.' The custom does not appear
to me an absurd one, but founded on the experience
of its utility ; nor can I think the superiority of the
Iliad supposed, but real.

' The moral of this poem,' says the Adventurer,
' is more extensively useful than that of the Iliad,
which, indeed, by displaying the dire effects of dis-
cord among rulers, may rectify the conduct of princes,
and may be called the manual of monarchs : whereas, the patience, the prudence, the wisdom, the tem-
perance, and fortitude of Ulysses, afford a pattern,
the utility of which is not confined within the compass of courts and palaces, but descends and dif-
fuses its influence over common life and daily practice.' Upon this argument, namely, that the affairs
which the Iliad treats of, are too far removed from
common life to be of service to common readers, is
grounded his principal objection to the practice before observed. Admitting the position to be true,
the conclusion does not necessarily follow. It is
universally allowed, that the doctrine of morality
has never been more forcibly inculcated, or its practice more strenuously and successfully recommended, than in the lofty tales and sublime language of
Eastern literature : they have been subjects of imitation to an Adventurer and a Rambler, and of admiration to all. The tendency of these tales is universally an incitement to virtue, by an unlimited display of the workings of Providence. Yet how far

removed are they from the business 'of common life and daily practice !'

Infinite merit is certainly due to the simplicity of the Odyssey. Yet is the Iliad by no means inferior in this particular. Even *inter reges atque tetrarchas* there is frequently room for it, and no opportunity is lost of introducing it. Whoever recollects how Andromache was employed, when from the top of the tower she beheld the fate of her husband, will in vain seek to find the simplicity of that passage which describes her employment any where equalled.

> ———— αλοχος δ' ουπω τι πεπυστο
> Εκτορος· ου γαρ οι τις ετητυμος αγγελος ελθων
> Ηγγειλ', οττι ρα οι ποσις εκτοθι μιμνε πυλαων·
> Αλλ' ηγ' ιστον υφαινε, μυχω δομου υψηλοιο,
> Διπλακα, μαρμαρεην, εν δε θρονα ποικιλ' επασσε·
> Κεκλετο δ' αμφιπολοισιν ευπλοκαμοις κατα δωμα
> Αμφι πυρι στησαι τριποδα μεγαν, οφρα πελοιτο
> Εκτορι θερμα λοετρα μαχης εκνοστησαντι·
> Νηπιη, ουδ' ενοησεν ο μιν μαλα τηλε λοετρων
> Χερσιν Αχιλληος δαμασεν γλαυκωπιρ Αθηνη.
> Κωκυτου δ' ηκουσε και οιμωγης απο πυργου,
> Της δ' ελελιχθη γυια, χαμαι δε οι εκπεσε κερκις.
>
> Il. xxii. 440.

But not as yet the fatal news had spread
To fair Andromache, of Hector dead, &c.

POPE, xxii. 462, &c.

Criticism has no language to describe the exquisite tenderness and simplicity of the

> Κεκλετο δ' αμφιπολοισιν ευπλοκαμοις κατα δωμα
> Αμφι πυρι στησαι τριποδα μεγαν, οφρα πελοιτο
> Εκτορι θερμα λοετρα, &c.

Mr. Pope's translation of which passage will give the English reader a very faint idea of the beauties of his original. The general originality of Thomson will not be impeached, if I subjoin a passage from his Winter, which bears a beautiful resemblance of the foregoing lines in Homer:

c 2

In vain for him the officious wife prepares
The fire fair blazing, and the vestment warm;
In vain his little children, peeping out
Into the mingling storm, demand their sire
With tears of artless innocence.   Alas!
Nor wife, nor children more shall he behold,
Nor friends, nor sacred home.

' If the fairest examples,' proceeds the Adventurer, ' ought to be placed before us in an age prone to imitation, if patriotism be preferable to implacability, if an eager desire to return to one's country and family, be more manly and noble, than an eager desire to be revenged of an enemy; then should our eyes be fixed rather on Ulysses than Achilles. Unexperienced minds, too easily captivated with the fire and fury of a gallant general, are apt to prefer courage to constancy, and firmness to humanity.' It is one of the acute Dr. Clarke's observations, that Homer has represented the character of Achilles, *qualis fuit, non qualis esse debuerit.* The remark, however obvious it may appear when made, would not, perhaps, have occurred to the mind of a common reader. The conduct of the son of Peleus is related, but not defended; the cause of virtue does not suffer by the exhibition of a character, in most respects amiable, in all illustrious, yet sometimes giving way to the gratifications of lust, and sometimes to an inordinate thirst for revenge. Its proper stigma is inflicted upon each deviation from virtue, by placing it in an odious light. His affectionate lamentation over his dead friend Patroclus, does not prevent the poet from stigmatizing the cruelty he exercised upon the slain Hector.

From a contemplation of the character of Ulysses and Achilles, very different sentiments arise. When we are observing the former, the mind is wrapped in unwearied admiration; it is scarce awakened to observation from a continued series of praiseworthy actions, but slumbers in the fulsomeness of perpetual panegyric. If we would examine thoroughly the character of the latter, the mind must be ever at work. There is much to praise, and much to condemn, through a variety of good and bad circumstances; we must 'pick our nice way.' His well-placed affection, his warm friendship, will create love; his revenge odium, and his cruelty abhorrence. Doubts will arise, and inquiry must be made, whether the one is more to be approved, or the other more to be avoided. Thus are we kept for ever on the watch: if our vigilance be for a moment abated, we have passed over some leading feature in the character of the hero, or lost the recital of some circumstance, by which we might determine whether the virtues or the vices of Achilles preponderate. When Ulysses comes forward, the mind is already prepared, and knows what to expect: he is either the πολυμητις διος Οδυσσευς, *the wise and divine Ulysses*, or the θεοις εναλιγκιος αυδην, *Ulysses godlike in voice.*—But upon the appearance of Achilles, we are uncertain whether he has broken his resolution of not going out to battle, or whether he is meditating the destruction of the Trojan bulwark.

The meeting between Achilles and Hector, which is terminated by the death of the latter, is replete with variety sufficient to arrest the attention of every one, and ornament sufficient to please every attention it engages. That defiance which each hurls at the other, marks the bravery of both; and when the latter falls, the prowess of the former is confirmed. The scene now alters. In his speech over the dead body of Hector, Achilles assigns to the gods the honour of his victory—επειδη τονδε ανδρα θεοι δαμασασθαι εδωκαν, &c.

Since now at length the powerful will of Heaven
The dire destroyer to our arm has given.—POPE, xxii. 275.

Yet this generosity cannot deprecate our abhorrence of the cruelty which follows. Hector is dragged at the wheels of his conqueror's chariot—

—Αμφι δε χαιται
Κυανεαι πιλναντο· καρη δ' απαν εν κονιησι
Κειτο παρος χαριεν·

'His hair is clotted, and that countenance, heretofore so beautiful, is all polluted in the dust.'

> Now lost is all that formidable air;
> The face divine, the long descending hair,
> Purple the ground, and streak the sable sand.
>
> POPE, xxii. 505.

This is done amid the lamentations of the Trojans, and it may be presumed the silent acquiescence of the Greeks. Yet the distress of this scene is still to be heightened. Who can bear the appearance and voice of the old king Priam, without heaping curses upon the author of his distress?—λισσομαι ανερα τουτον ατασθαλον οβριμοεργον, &c.

> I, only I, will issue from your walls,
> (Guide or companion, friends, I ask ye none)
> And bow before the murderer of my son.
>
> POPE, xxii. 531.

'The remaining reasons why the Odyssey is equal,' says the Adventurer, 'if not superior to the Iliad, and why more peculiarly proper for the perusal of youth, are because the great variety of events and scenes it contains, interest and engage the attention more than the Iliad; because characters and images drawn from familiar life are more useful to the generality of readers, and are also more difficult to be drawn; and because the conduct of this poem (considered as the most perfect of epopees) is more artful and judicious than that of the other.' The first of these remaining reasons, namely, that the Odyssey must interest and engage the attention more

than the Iliad, I fear is a declaration which will go
near to overturn what is advanced in the beginning
of the critique, ' that unexperienced minds, too
easily captivated with the fire and fury of a gallant
general, are apt to prefer courage to constancy, and
firmness to humanity.' The difficulty of drawing a
character is perhaps no where so happily surmounted as in the 2d book of the Iliad, wherein he gives
an account of Thersites.

Φολκος εην, χωλος δ' ετερον ποδα, τω δε οι ωμω
Κυρτω, επι στηθος συνοχωκοτε· αυταρ υπερθε
Φοξος εην κεφαλην, ψεδνη δ' επενηνοθε λαχνη.
Εχθιστος δ' Αχιληι μαλιστ' ην ηδ' Οδυσηι,
Τω γαρ νεικειεσκε. Τοτ' αυ Αγαμεμνονι διω
Οξεα κεκληγως λεγ' ονειδεα· τω δ' αρ Αχαιοι
Εκπαγλως κοτεοντο, νεμεσσηθεν τ' ενι θυμω.
Αυταρ ο μακρα βοων, Αγαμεμνονα νεικεε μυθω.

His figure such as might his soul proclaim;
One eye was blinking, and one leg was lame.
POPE, ii. 263.

This may perhaps be called rather a description of
his person than a delineation of his character. Yet,
if with this description we take in the few preceding
lines, the art of the poet has left us ignorant of
nothing which is passing in the mind of Thersites.
Providence has been kindly parsimonious in the production of such objects, yet they have come within
the notice of most people. The conduct of the
Odyssey may be more reducible to rule, but the
Iliad abounds with the sublimer beauties.

Whoever is acquainted with the Ajax and Phi-
loctetes of Sophocles, and the contention between
Ajax and Ulysses of Ovid, will be convinced that
Homer's character of Ulysses is drawn to an excess
con amore, and that of Achilles with fidelity. On
the one hand, he will observe the flattering fondness
of the painter; on the other, he will approve the in-
flexible veracity of the historian. MONRO.

N° 3. SATURDAY, MARCH 31, 1787.

Arcades ambo.—VIRG.

SLAVES at Athens, who had been guilty of theft, were, in order to publish their disgrace and infamy, branded in the forehead with two letters, and were thence called γραμματοι or *literati*.

When I acknowledge my obligations to two distinguished *literati*, whose letters will compose the substance of this paper, I caution my classical readers against supposing that I use the word in its original Athenian sense.

' TO THE AUTHOR OF THE OLLA PODRIDA.

' DEAR BROTHER,   London, March, 1787.

' The familiarity with which I address you, will, I think, be sufficiently justified, when I inform you, that I am an author as well as yourself. Our lines of business differ, indeed. Your care seems to be in endeavouring to entertain your readers with productions of the lighter cast, while I am engaged in graver duties; troublesome, indeed, to myself, but of the utmost importance to mankind. You must know, I am the mouth from which many of our pastors and instructors deliver their oracles. In short, my office is to write sermons for young divines; which (such is my zeal for religion) I distribute at threepence each, or 2s. 9d. per dozen. After the expenses of printing, &c. are defrayed, my gains, as you may suppose, are very small. Yet, small as they are, Sir, I am satisfied, while my conscience, without flattering, tells me I have deserved, if not obtained, a reputation. One of my sermons (it was printed in a type which might be mistaken for hand-writing, price only 1s.) procured the purchaser of it a lectureship in the Borough: to be sure, the gentleman had a main good voice, which he did not possess for nothing. But what is the sage without the goose?

'Another gentleman, a doctor, who wrote rather grave sermons, being much smitten with a young lady, who objected to him on account of his gravity, applied to me for a sermon suited to his circumstances. I took his case into consideration, and provided him with a discourse so lively, that he carried off the lady in triumph in less than three weeks. Nobody slept; the people were very attentive, and stared a good deal.

'While I was busy in composing this sermon, a few evenings ago, for the doctor, three young divines, my customers, rapped at my door. Compliments having been on each side paid and received, they were seated. When I informed them of the business I was engaged in, from what reason I know not, I found in all of them a promptitude to laughter, which was irksome to me; but as every now and then some observation was made, which was the specious cause of their merriment, I was unwilling to suppose they meant a direct insult: but at last, I had too manifest a proof of their intentions to deride me. My candle wanted snuffing: the snuffers were not to be found. I have no bell in my room, but am accustomed to summon my landlady, who lives under me, by the stamp of my foot. I now gave the young rogues occasion to banter me. One told me, I reminded him of Pompey the Great, who declared before the senate, that he could raise legions by the motion of his foot; but that I was superior, in performing what Pompey found he could not. Another drily congratulated me upon the acquisition of a

place in the stamp-office : the third (who was determined to have his fling at me, though what he said
had nothing to do with the present business) begged
I would give him my opinion of South's Sermons ;
and observed, that he had that morning turned off
his tailor for having detected him in cabbaging. I
disdained to make any reply to the grossness of
their wit, nor did I even reproach them with ingra-
titude. I neither reminded the one of the charity
sermon which got him so much applause ; nor the
other, of the funeral sermon which set his congregation a roaring : but to me they are obliged for most
of their discourses, and all their reputation. To be
sure, the slip I made in transcribing South's sermon
was unlucky. But am I for that to be made miserable for ever ? Am I for that to lose my reputation ;
and must I return to my old trade of stay-making? Do,
good brother, consider the dignity of our profession,
and put me in a way of mitigating the rigour of some
of my critical customers, and regaining the favours
of others, which I have lost by an unfortunate cab-
bage, or the laughter of an audience, when it was
the intention of the preacher that they should be
grave. Render me this piece of service, and I will
write your funeral sermon, which you shall inspect,
and, if you please, alter before you die.

  ' Bound, together with you, in the service of the
public, believe me yours sincerely,

                              HABAKKUK CANTWELL.

  ' P. S. If any gentleman agrees with me for sermons by the great, I give him my lecture on delivery
for nothing, and for my essay on pulpit-oratory charge
him only one shilling and sixpence, which to common
customers is two shillings. I exchange his old sermons for new, at half-price.

  ' N. B. My landlady has requested that I will take

every handsome opportunity of informing her neighbours and the public, that she sells corn-plaster, and
really very good; for I have used it. No. 13, St.
—— street, Petty France. To prevent mistakes, a
blue lamp over the door. Mr. Cantwell is always
at home, except on Sundays, and then is to be spoken
with at the Admiral Rodney, Islington.'

I am unwilling to quarrel with the familiarity of
my brother Cantwell, lest, as he in all probability
deals in the proverbs and the *noverbs*, he should remark, that I lay myself open to the application of the
well-known, ' Two of a trade can never agree.'   His
generosity in making a present of his lecture to his
customers, reminds me of the lame man, who cried,
' Come, buy my gingerbread, and I will give you a
dram.' It is true he gave his dram, but made you
pay sixpence for a gingerbread nut: so the famous
Dr. Leo cures his patients gratis, and only charges
half-a-crown for his box of salve.

' To the Author of the Olla Podrida.

' SIR,

' I herewith send you a short history of myself. I
did once keep a theme shop in a university, which
shall be nameless, where I served undergraduates
with exercises of every kind, having men under me
whom I employed in the different branches of the
trade. These were not your handicraftsmen, your
starvelings, and your nick-bottoms; but, as I may
say, they were *eruditi togati homines*, learned men,
men of the gown. To each I allotted their different
departments; here were your translators, your de-
clamation-spinners, and your weavers of Lent-epi-
gram. By the labours of these gentry, whom I paid
by the piece, I got a decent livelihood; but as I
thought my talents considerably improved by habitual

commerce with books and bookish men, I resolved
to shake off all encumbrance, and seek a place where
I might give play to my abilities, and obtain a share
of reputation as well as a livelihood. It is now about
a twelvemonth since, that, in conformity to this resolution, I opened a neat and convenient shop, not
far from the bottom of the Haymarket, where I deal
out to customers of all sorts, whatever they may want
in the literary way, at the lowest prices.

'I have by me, in the poetic line, every thing that
can be named, from an acrostic to an epic poem. I
have sun-risings and sun-settings for all persons,
places, and seasons. Not like Mr. Bickerstaff's,
confined to this or that condition : but I have the
milk-maid's sun-rise, the cobbler's sun-rise, the politician's sun-rise, the poet's or common sun-rise,
with proper sun-sets to match them. I have storms
for seamen, and storms for landsmen ; not to mention a few hail storms, squalls of wind, &c. &c. I
have similes from Arcadia for pastoral writers ; metaphors for people of quality, in Joe Miller's true
sense of the word, such as you never *met-a-fore*; and
a bundle of tropes unsorted, consisting of metonomy,
aposiopesis, synecdoche, &c. for epic poets and son-
neteers. I have a fine soliloquy, supposed to have
been uttered by Nahum Tate upon his death-bed :
it is not in a strain of rant, but so tender—it would
do your heart good to hear how my shop boy does roar
when I read it to him.

'In the way of prose, I have jokes for disbanded
statesmen, elegantly-turned compliments suited to
all occasions, and panegyrics applicable to all people, provided they are high in the world ; an essay
on the baneful effects of intemperance and charcoal ;
a loose parcel of sentences for mottos ; a few knowing phrases to be used at races ; with a file of conun-
drums to make the ladies laugh—the latter are well

adapted to the mouth of any gentleman who has a remarkable good set of teeth. Of the graver kind, I have two sermons, which smack pretty well of the high church; a two-shilling pamphlet upon the rise and fall of the tucker:—this is in black letter, and treats of an invention of our ancestors, which has been unhappily lost. I have looked in Pancirolus, and all the books of that sort, and can find no mention of it; it is, therefore, a considerable curiosity.

'I have speeches suited to members of parliament in all trying situations; whether they are about to consult their constituents through the medium of a hogshead of claret, or to descant upon an infringement of the game laws: some pithy sarcasms upon country members, who have been often ridiculed, but never properly handled; an essay on matrimony; and an elaborate treatise on the use and abuse of the parenthesis in modern composition. Who knows, Mr. ——, but I may be able to serve you one of these days, when you have been idle, or are put to it for a joke? I say nothing, but there is nobody I would sooner oblige. I will send you some specimens of the different works I have mentioned; and shall hope, at least, to meet with your approbation, if not your custom.

I am, Sir, yours, &c.

MONRO.   POLUMATHES.'

N° 4.   SATURDAY, APRIL 7, 1787.

> Deferar in vicum vendentem thus et odores,
> Et piper, et quidquid chartis amicitur ineptis.—HORACE.

> Perhaps in the same open basket laid,
> Down to the street together be convey'd;
> Where pepper, odours, frankincense are sold,
> And all small wares in wretched rhymes unroll'd.—FRANCIS.

IT is melancholy to reflect on the unhappy circumstances which have frequently attended the deaths of authors. If we turn over the pages of literary history, we shall find, that although many have enjoyed the gratification of hearing their own praises, and some have even basked in the sunshine of opulent patronage, yet their deaths have been often obscure, and sometimes disastrous. Cicero fell a victim to party-rage; Sidney expired in the field of battle; Crichton fell by assassination; and Otway perished by famine.

The fate of books is oftentimes similar to that of authors. The flattery of dedications, and the testimony of friends, are frequently interposed in vain to force them into popularity and applause. It is not the fashion of the present day to indulge the hangman with the amusement of committing books to the flames; yet they are in many instances condemned to a more inglorious destiny. The grocer, the chemist, and the tallow-chandler, with 'ruthless and unhallowed hands,' tear whole libraries in pieces and feel as little compunction on the occasion, as the Thracian ladies did when they dismembered Orpheus. The leaves are distributed among their customers with sundry articles of trade that have little connexion with classical fragments, whilst the tradesman, like the Sibyl, cares not a farthing what becomes of them.

> Nunquam deinde cavo volitantia prendere saxo,
> Nec revocare situs, aut jungere carmina curat.—VIRGIL.

I was led into this train of thought by receiving a pound of sugar from my neighbour Tim Teartitle, the grocer, wrapped up in a sheet of letter-press. Tim deals so largely in books, that he has many more than are sufficient for his own use, with which he very bountifully obliges the literati in foreign parts. I remember, just before the American war broke out, my curiosity was excited to know what a large hogshead, which stood at his door, contained. I found, on close examination, that it was filled with old pamphlets, most of them on subjects of liberty, non-conformity, and whiggism, which Tim was going to ship off for a Yankee shop-keeper in New-England. Whatever sage politicians may have said to the contrary, it is not at all to be doubted, that the importation of this cargo spread the wildfire of rebellion among the Bostonians, and was the sole cause of the late bloody and expensive war. Although my neighbour Tim is no scholar by profession, yet it is astonishing what a progress he has made in books: he has finished a complete set of the General Councils, and is now hard at work upon the Ante-Nicene Fathers, whom he cuts up with greater expedition than Dr. Priestley himself. Perhaps more logic and metaphysics have passed through his hands than Lord Monboddo ever saw. He would have been a long time in dispatching a set of French Reviews, had he not begun upon them when the price of coffee was reduced. The other day some young sparks, who belong to a celebrated academy, where every thing is taught, brought him a parcel of Latin classics. He tore off the covers with as much sang-froid as a nymph

of Billingsgate strips an oyster of its shell, and
bought Horace and Virgil for three-halfpence per
pound. He observed, with a sapient look, ‘ That as
for your Virgilii's translation into Latin, I reckon it
no better than waste paper; but if it had been Mr.
Dryden's History of the Trojan Horse, I would have
kept it for my own reading.’

I have been told by learned men, that it is a
question much debated in the universities, whether
the ‘ place ought to agree with the thing placed.’
Now after all that serious meditation which so abstruse a point requires, I am determined to decide in
the affirmative. For who cannot see the propriety,
or rather (as Parson Square would say) the fitness of
things, in wrapping up a cheesecake in a pastoral,
sugar-candy in a dedication, and gunpowder in a
sermon on the 5th of November?

There never was a time when learning forced itself
so much into notice as it does at present. You can no
more walk a hundred yards in any street, or go into
any house, without seeing some display of it, than
you can turn a corner in London without seeing a
beggar, or hear a sailor talk without swearing. A
man of fashion keeps up his acquaintance with his
alphabet, by playing at the noble game of te-totum,
or risking his fortune at an E O table. Book-stalls
furnish history; the walls of houses poetry; hand-
bills medicine; fire-screens geography; and clocks
morality. These are the channels which convey to
the porter the knowledge of the constitution, to the
apprentice the art of rhyming, to members of parliament an acquaintance with our India settlements,
and to the fat alderman wise sayings.

For my own part, I am not satisfied with such
vulgar means of growing learned, but love to follow
literature into her more secret recesses. Fortunately, chance has furnished me with the means of

doing this, without being driven to the immense bore of poring over books, which would only produce the effects of a dose of opium. I have a trunk, which, like the dagger of Hudibras, may be applied to more purposes than one. It is lined with several sheets of the Royal Register, and of course contains much edifying information. During my travels, I watch my trunk with the same fond anxiety which Sancho used to feel for his beloved Dapple. On my arrival at an inn, after having studied the most curious manuscript in the house, the bill of fare, I unlock my magazine of linen and learning, and feast upon delicious scraps of characters, until more substantial food is set upon the table. When I travel in company, my associates complain of my taking an unreasonable time to equip myself. They are not aware, that frequently, whilst they think I am fluctuating between boots and shoes, I am conjecturing what the initial letters of my fragment stand for, and that, instead of changing my linen, I am shifting from the Duke of Marlborough to Lord Chatham.

To those who wish not to forget all that their school-masters taught them, this sort of light reading is to be recommended. It would be no bad plan if all genteel people would furnish their trunks, portmanteaus, caravans, and band-boxes, with the beauties of some author that suits their taste. If the beau monde should be afraid of injuring their eyes by these studies, Mademoiselle Abigail, or Monsieur Valet de Chambre, had better be deputed to read *trunk*-lectures to them. Hoyle on Whist will answer extremely well for old ladies; Tom Jones or Joseph Andrews for boarding-school misses; Ecton's Thesaurus, or the Art of Shooting Flying, for parsons: Paterson's Book of Roads for lawyers on the circuit; and Phillidore on Chess, for the gentlemen of the army.

Pedants may object, that if the above plan should become general, the works of the learned will be no longer treasured up in the libraries of the great. But let them not be alarmed; for they may be certain, that whilst books are considered by a refined age as a species of ornamental furniture, and supply the place of the *classics in wood*, they will not be driven from their present posts. There is, it must be confessed, great reason to be alarmed at the destruction which threatens some branches of literature. Innumerable enemies are constantly on the watch, to annihilate insipid novels, scurrilous satires, party pamphlets, and indecent songs. If they chance to attract the public eye for a week or two, they cannot escape that destiny which their authors were too much dazzled with their own charming productions to foresee. As weeds by their decay fertilize the soil from which they sprung, so these flimsy and noxious publications do great service to society, by lighting a pipe, embracing a tallow-candle, or forming the basis of a minced-pie.

Q.   KETT.

Nº 5. SATURDAY, APRIL 14, 1787.

Μισω σοφιστην οστις ουκ αυτω σοφει.—Gr. Prov.

THERE is no species of science whose utility is more generally allowed than that which is called knowledge of the world, the safeguard of the prudent, the manual of the cunning, and sometimes the instrument of virtue. It has been often remarked, that men of acknowledged abilities and great literary merits, have been in general found more deficient in this kind of knowledge than the illiterate and the vulgar. Some have ranked this acquisition so low, as to have supposed it unworthy such men's attention; others have, perhaps, erroneously conjectured, that it was too high for their attainment; and others again, with more shadow of reason, have ascribed their want of it to the imperfection of human nature.

Since the excellence and superiority of this attainment is acknowledged by all, it is not to be wondered at, if the acquisition of it engages the attention and pursuit of all.

It may not be improper to ascertain, as near as possible, the meaning of the term *knowledge of the world*, which with every different class of men has a different acceptation. With some people it means, what has been called a knavish form of understanding, abounding in tricks of low cunning, and pregnant with stratagems, by which a person advances his own interest, without regard to the ruin of the unwary or the contempt of the upright. The man of trade, whom his own arts or his own industry have enriched, is sufficiently convinced, that to his knowledge of the world he is indebted for his present exemption from business, for the enjoyment of his villa, and the envy of his neighbourhood. In his great veneration for this kind of knowledge, he forgets that the same arts which expedite the acquisition of wealth, frequently supply temptations to impair honesty.

Some arrive at this knowledge, by living with an opera-singer at Paris, bringing home the name of a noted Italian ballet-master, or wearying out the attention of their yawning friends with indefinite and unsatisfactory accounts of the Escurial. To some a more easy path towards the acquiring know-

ledge is open: they may learn, without leaving
London, with what ease the ace of spades will convey an estate from one honourable family to another; of how little moment it is, whe ncompared
with a rational amusement of a serious game of
whist, whether a wife be made unhappy, or a family
ruined.

Some, who are not fond of parting with their
money without any gratification, have been prudent
enough to stipulate for sport in exchange; well satisfied they repair to that repository of the arts and
sciences, Newmarket, and are handsomely recom-
pensed by a good gallop for the loss of their whole
fortune.

It is knowledge of the world which directs the
cheesemonger's wife in her choice of a gown, and
the putting up of her pickles; it determines whether her cap shall be like Mrs. Cheshire's or Mrs.
Tape's; whether her Sunday's ride shall convey her
to the Angel at Highgate, or to the Pack-horse at
Turnham-green. Knowledge of the world persuades
the spendthrift, that in expense alone consists the
scavoir vivre; and teaches the usurer to withhold
his loan till the premium is doubled. The increase
of his knowledge begets that comfortable contempt
which each class entertains for the other; it sup-
ports the man of substance in his condemnation of
poverty, and instructs the man of pleasure to despise the sons of mechanism and tallow.

It is knowledge of the world by which the man
of fashion acquires a readiness in the different forms
of salutation; the proper reserve with which he
treats an inferior; and the skilful adulation with
which he approaches the fool greater than himself.

To his knowledge of the world the clerical soli-
citor is obliged, while he evades the penalties in-

curred by simoniacal contracts, flies from the vigilance of episcopal inquiry, and is mean enough to shear the flock which he is too proud to feed.

The sceptic in religion discovers his knowledge of the world by asserting a natural right to think for himself; by searching, with eager inquiry, after what must be for ever before his eyes; and doubting the truth of that which nature insists upon ' through all her works.'

It is, forsooth, an accurate knowledge of the world which prompts the atheist to inform his hearers that the duties of religion are impositions upon the weak and credulous, the contrivances of ambition, the clogs and impediments to the progress of real merit.

It is this salutary knowledge of the world which assists the libertine in his career, and gives vigour to the arm of the suicide.

This boasted wisdom then, by which the tradesman acquires wealth, the minion of fashion the notice of his peers, the sceptic reputation, and the libertine encouragement, is too high for the attainment only of men of abilities, science, and literature! This is surely a position to which no logical fallacy can give the appearance of truth. Is it probable, that the same man, who can successfully combat the insidious arguments of schismatic theologists, should become the dupe of a low-minded and designing mechanic? Or shall he, who can with accuracy examine the claims of the impostor Mahomet, bow down before the superior wisdom of a tricking dedler?

It is from an honest benevolence of heart, the peculiar concomitant of an enlightened mind, which neglects to fortify itself against attacks it has never provoked, and disdains to suspect the injury it has never felt, that men of superior talents frequently fall into the snares of these sagacious sons of prudence.

It is not to be wondered at, that they whose attention has been diverted from the concerns of the world to objects of a higher nature, should perform those offices which are necessary to society with less skill than others, whose lives have been consumed in the constant intercourse with mankind, and the noise and bustle of business. In the performance of these offices, the frequent superiority of ignorance over learning is evident and confessed. The former oftentimes effects with ease, what the latter in vain attempts with awkwardness and timidity; awkwardness, arising from a bashful mind, and timidity from the consciousness of its own defects.

Yet let those who excel in worldly wisdom bear their triumph with moderation, when they are reminded, that wealth, which only gratifies the avarice of its possessor, without being the instrument of his benevolence, is neither honourable nor ornamental; and that power, for which ambition pants, only shews itself illustrious, when it is exerted to suppress injustice, and to protect innocence.

MONRO.

N° 6.   SATURDAY, APRIL 21, 1787.

Credula turba sumus.

THE character of the late king of Prussia, together with the residence of Dr. Katterfelto, and other heroes of that country in England, have contributed to raise in the minds of many of our countrymen a very high and splendid idea of that nation of philosophers, warriors, and physicians.

I was passing, not long ago, through Holborn with a friend, whom I had all my life mistaken for a man of sense, when a printed bill of Dr. Katterfelto's was put into our hands, and soon after the doctor himself, in a shabby kind of chariot, wisked by us. 'Is that,' exclaimed my friend, 'an equipage suitable to the character and condition of a brother to a colonel in the King of Prussia's life-guards? Ought he to be reduced to the necessity every day of reminding the public of his situation, his dignity, and his quality? Is it not scandalous, that he who has done such signal services to all the princes and potentates of Europe, should be suffered in this humiliating manner to supplicate the attendance of gentlemen and ladies upon his exhibition at only one shilling each? Oh, Mr. ***, I am sorry to say it, we are an envious nation, and willing only to favour those whom we despise. The French send over their Vestris, their dancing-dogs, and wheedle us out of our money, and then skip off with it; the Italians,—but we will not talk of them, for I shall be in a passion—while this honest Dr. Katterfelto can with difficulty obtain a livelihood. There is Dr. Leo again, who has performed such and so many extraordinary cures in most of the King of Prussia's camps, to say nothing of his table in Covent-garden, where I myself have felt the salutary effects of his advice. I am really ashamed, Sir, suppose these gentlemen should ever go back, as they have often threatened, to their own country, what must become of our national reputation? The wonderful doctor would take away his cats with him, and the tall regiment would laugh at us.'

My friend was so serious in his harangue, that I would not hazard offending him by ridicule; but I could not help hinting my doubts as to the truth of the assertions, which these gentry are very apt to make.

Upon my return home, I immediately dispatched a messenger to the shop of my ingenious and valuable friend and correspondent Mr. Polumathes, requesting that he would send me by the bearer a short essay on that benevolent credulity, by which our friend John Bull is so distinguished, and so deceived; with which I purposed to conclude this paper. My messenger brought back the following answer, replete with that candour and good sense for which Mr. P. is so justly celebrated.

'DEAR SIR,   Friday morning.

'The commission you have been so kind as to favour me with, highly flatters me. It raises my idea of your discernment, and my own abilities; but the reason why I cannot execute it so faithfully as I could wish, is briefly as follows. Some time ago, it was, I know not by what enemies to the state, industriously strewed in the common ear, and was believed by the herd, that the lake of Geneva was filled with gin. Now this I knew to be a vulgar error, and to prevent its evil consequences by emigration, and to put a little money in my own pocket, I gave the world a pamphlet on the subject. Herein I sufficiently pointed out to my honest countrymen those inconveniences, into which they were too easily led by their credulity. I assured them the report was a false one; and, moreover, that they might get as good gin at the Two Brewers, or the White Horse Cellar, as Geneva could produce. You will not be surprised if I add, that in this pamphlet I exhausted on the subject all the rhetoric I had in my shop; and indeed left myself so bare of argument, that I had not enough by me to answer a trifling squib which was written in ridicule of my work.

' Receive my thanks for the honour you have done me, and believe me on this, and all other occasions, your servant at command,

                        MICHAEL POLUMATHES.'

Such being the answer of my friend Mr. Michael Polumathes, my intention of giving to the world a treatise upon so interesting a subject is frustrated; and I have room left to recommend to their notice the letters of two other correspondents.

' TO THE AUTHOR OF THE OLLA PODRIDA.

  ' DEAR SIR,

' I should be very much obliged to you or any person who would define to me the meaning of a very common phrase, "He's a dry fellow." It is a mode of expression which all people use, and many, I dare say, understand: I own, I do not. As I was coming out of Whitehall, a few Sundays ago, I met a friend at the door, who asked me what the doctor had been preaching about: I told him, as near as I could guess, about twenty-five minutes. He immediately put me down, as he said, for a dry fellow. It was in vain that I assured him I was not dry: he insisted upon it I was, and he should reckon me so as long as I lived. I was some time after relating to him what I thought a *bon-mot* of a man, who, being advised to enlarge his house, because (as his adviser observed) he had not room to swing a cat, simply replied, "I don't want to swing a cat." He heard my story, and then affirmed, that I had a set of the *dryest* acquaintance of any man he knew. I repeatedly endeavoured to bring him to an explanation, but to no purpose: all I could get from him was, "a cursed dry fellow—a dry dog indeed."

XLI.   E

Now if this phrase has no meaning, it should be abolished: if it has any, I should take it as a great favour if it might be no longer concealed from the vulgar; of which I confess myself one.

JERRY SIMPLE.'

'TO THE AUTHOR OF THE OLLA PODRIDA.

'SIR,

' Sauntering along the road the other day, I came to a small inn, where all was bustle and confusion by the arrival of some great family, with their numerous retinue; but what claimed most attention was the accident of a favourite dog, who was trod on by one of the horses turning short; whether it was by chance, or whether it again proved that a favourite has no friends, was not for me to decide: a glass of brandy was called for: a common gill, enough to warm a poor man in a cold morning, was rejected as insufficient; and nothing would do but a tumbler full, to bathe Pero's foot in: it was afterward rubbed with Friar's balsam, bound up with rags, and committed to the care of Mrs. Betty, to travel in the coach with her. I admire compassion wherever I see it exerted through the wide sphere of sensitive life; but our refinement may be carried too far, and that sympathizing attention which humanity demands, be squandered on the brute creation. I knew an old maiden lady, whose tears could tenderly flow at the relation of the sufferings of a cat, but who did not exhibit any active benevolence at the call of the wants of her poor or suffering neighbours. Yet she could readily excuse herself by unremitting attention to her favourite animals. Let them be provided for according to their condition; yet we must remember that there are duties of humanity belonging to a higher class; and we shall find but small excuse in the judgment of enlightened reason, if we urge our regard to inferior obligations, while those of a superior kind are neglected.   I am, yours, &c.   VIATOR.

MONRO, except the last Letter by AGUTTER.

N° 7. SATURDAY, APRIL 28, 1787.

Servatâ semper lege et ratione loquendi.—JUVENAL.

THE different writers, who have obliged the world with memoirs of Dr. Johnson, all agree to inform us, that he esteemed conversation to be the comfort of life. He himself, indeed, in an Idler, has not scrupled to compare it to a bowl of that liquor, which, under the direction of Mr. Brydone, so deservedly engaged the attention of the Sicilian clergy; and in the composition of which, while the spirit is duly tempered by water, and the acid sufficiently corrected by sugar, the ingredients wonderfully conspire to form the most delicious beverage known among mortals.

But whether it be that the requisites for producing conversation, like those for making punch, are not always to be had, or are not good in their kind, or not properly mixed, certain it is that in the former case, as in the latter, the operation does not at all times succeed to the satisfaction of the company; nothing being more common than to hear persons complaining, that after many hours passed in this way, they have found neither improvement nor entertainment.

Without study or method, I shall set down such

thoughts as may occur to my mind, on this most interesting subject.

That conversation may answer the ends for which
it was designed, the parties, who are to join in it,
must come together with a determined resolution
to please and to be pleased. If a man feels that
an east wind has rendered him dull and sulky, he
should by all means stay at home till the wind
changes, and not be troublesome to his friends; for
dulness is infectious, and one sour face will make
many, as one cheerful countenance is soon productive of others. If two gentlemen desire to quarrel,
it should not be done in a company met to enjoy the
pleasures of conversation. Let a stage be erected
for the purpose, in a proper place, to which the ju-
risdiction of the Middlesex magistrates doth not
reach. There let Martin and Mendoza mount, accompanied by Ben and Johnson, and attended by
the amateurs, who delight to behold blows neatly
laid in, ribs and jaw-bones elegantly broken, and
eyes sealed up with delicacy and address. It is obvious, for these reasons, that he, who is about to
form a conversation party, should be careful to in-
vite men of congenial minds, and of similar ideas
respecting the entertainment of which they are to
partake, and to which they must contribute.

With gloomy persons, gloomy topics likewise
should be (as indeed they will be) excluded, such as
ill-health, bad weather, bad news, or forebodings of
such, &c. &c. To preserve the temper calm and
pleasant, it is of unspeakable importance, that we
always accustom ourselves through life to make the
best of things, to view them on their bright side, and
so represent them to others, for our mutual comfort
and encouragement. Few things (especially if, as
Christians, we take the other world into the account)
but have a bright side : diligence and practice will

easily find it. Perhaps there is no circumstance better calculated than this, to render conversation equally pleasing and profitable.

In the conduct of it, be not eager to interrupt others, or uneasy at being yourself interrupted; since you speak either to amuse or instruct the company, or to receive those benefits from it. Give all, therefore, leave to speak in turn. Hear with patience, and answer with precision. Inattention is ill manners: it shews contempt; and contempt is never forgiven.

Trouble not the company with your own private concerns, as you do not love to be troubled with those of others. Yours are as little to them as theirs are to you. You will need no other rule whereby to judge of this matter.

Contrive, but with dexterity and propriety, that each person may have an opportunity of discoursing on the subject with which he is best acquainted. He will be pleased, and you will be informed. By observing this rule, every one has it in his power to assist in rendering conversation agreeable; since, though he may not choose, or be qualified to say much himself, he can propose questions to those who are able to answer them.

Avoid stories, unless short, pointed, and quite *a-propos*. 'He who deals in them,' says Swift, 'must either have a very large stock, or a good memory, or must often change his company.' Some have a set of them strung together like onions: they take possession of the conversation, by an early introduction of one; and then you must have the whole *rope*, and there is an end of every thing else, perhaps, for that meeting, though you may have heard all twenty times before.

Talk often, but not long. The talent of haranguing in private company is insupportable. Senators and barristers are apt to be guilty of this fault; and members, who never harangue in the house, will often do it out of the house: if the majority of the company be naturally silent, or cautious, the conversation will flag, unless it be often renewed by one among them, who can start new subjects. Forbear, however, if possible, to broach a second, before the first is out, lest your stock should not last, and you should be obliged to come back to the old barrel. There are those who will repeatedly cross upon, and break into the conversation, with a fresh topic, till they have touched upon all, and exhausted none. Economy here is necessary for most people.

Laugh not at your own wit and humour: leave that to the company.

When the conversation is flowing in a serious and useful channel, never interrupt it by an ill-timed jest. The stream is scattered, and cannot be again collected.

Discourse not in a whisper, or half voice, to your next neighbour: it is ill-breeding, and in some degree a fraud; conversation-stock being, as one has well observed, a joint and common property.

In reflections on absent people, go no farther than you would go if they were present. ‘ I resolve,’ says Bishop Beveridge, ‘ never to speak of a man's virtues before his face, nor of his faults behind his back:’ a golden rule! the observation of which, would, at one stroke, banish flattery and defamation from the earth.

Conversation is effected by circumstances, which, at first sight, may appear trifling, but really are not so. Some, who continue dumb while seated, become at once loquacious when they are (as the senatorial phrase is) *upon their legs:* others, whose powers languish in a close room, recover themselves on putting their heads into fresh air, as a shrovetide cock does when his head is put into fresh earth : a turn or two in the garden makes them good company. There is a magic sometimes in a large circle which fascinates those who compose it into silence ; and nothing can be done, or, rather, nothing can be said, till the introduction of a card-table breaks up the spell, and releases the valiant knights and fair damsels from captivity. A table indeed, of any kind, considered as a centre of union, is of eminent service to conversation at all times ; and never do we more sensibly feel the truth of that old philosophical axiom, that nature ' abhors a vacuum,' than upon its removal. I have been told, that even in the Blue-stocking Society, formed solely for the purpose of conversation, it was found, after repeated trials, impossible to get on, without one card-table. In that same venerable society, when the company is too widely extended to engage in the same conversation, a custom is said to prevail—and a very excellent one it is—that every gentleman, upon his entrance, selects his partner, as he would do at a ball ; and when the conversation-dance is gone down, the company change partners, and begin afresh. Whether these things be so or not, most certain it is, that the lady or the gentleman deserves well of the society, who can devise any method, whereby so valuable an amusement can be heightened and improved.—Z.　　　　　　　　Bishop Horne.

Nº 8.　SATURDAY, MAY 5, 1787.

Cui dicas sæpe videto.

There are many persons in the world, whose wit and whose judgment, like two parallel lines, never

meet; who are still neither deficient in wit, nor destitute of judgment. An improper use of the former,
or a temporary absence of the latter, usually renders
both ineffectual.

To what purpose is judgment employed in making
proper observations, and forming proper opinions;
or wit called forth to illustrate those observations,
or display those opinions in all the ornament of well-
turned language or elegant allusion, if they are, perchance, exhibited before an audience, prejudiced
against the speaker, unwilling to attend to him, or
incapable of understanding him? In such a case,
the judgment must have been lulled to sleep, and the
wit thrown away.

To my reflections upon this subject, I was led by
a circumstance which not long ago happened to myself. An ingenious friend, with whom I was conversing, addressed to me some strictures upon a periodical publication, which, he observed, was then
carrying on in Oxford, called the ' Olla Podrida.'
After expatiating for some time in general terms,
upon the small probability of success attendant on
such a plan, owing to the political distraction of the
nation, the exhausted state of materials necessary
for such a work, and, in short, the general decay of
readers and writers; he descended to be more particular in his criticisms; he could not help observing,
that the characteristic of the first number was an affectation of modesty, and of the second an affectation of learning. ' Why else,' added he, ' was not
the full translation of each passage in Homer admitted from Mr. Pope?' He then concluded his
critique with some happy sarcasms upon Monsieur
l'Auteur, at which he laughed violently, and I accompanied him as well as I could. I avoided entering into a minute defence of the gentleman, at whose
expense we had been so agreeably entertained, lest I

should discover myself to be too much interested in his behalf; but was content to observe, that it might be more difficult to write an introductory paper than we were aware of, and, with regard to the admission of Mr. Pope's translation of each passage, that the paper appeared so full, as necessarily to exclude either that or the original.

'Besides,' added he (recovering himself from the convulsion of merriment into which his own friendly ideas had betrayed him), ' upon such a subject as the Iliad or Odyssey, who cares what the Adventurer has said, or what the Olla Podrida has to say? Every body knows that each is a model of different excellence, that the former is the work of genius in the full and vigorous exertions of all its powers, and the latter bears evident marks of the poet's having arrived at a maturity of judgment, though, at the same time, he discovers the decay of age.' I acquiesced more with silence than satisfaction in what I heard my friend advance. Had he known me for the author, while his conscientious adherence to truth might have extorted the same opinions from him, he would have been prevented from triumphing in the insolence of wit. This tribute he would have paid to delicacy. When he reads the eighth number of the Olla Podrida, he will probably agree in opinion with me, that those thoughts have been conceived in an unlucky moment which are expressed in an improper one. He will, likewise, be reminded, that people are inclined to entertain little opinion of that judgment which controverts their own sentiments, and little relish for that wit by which themselves become ridiculous.

I shall solace myself with the assurance Mr. Addison has given us, ' That there is, and ever will be, justice enough in the world, to afford patronage and protection for those who endeavour to advance truth and virtue, without any regard to the passions and prejudices of any particular cause and faction*.'

But lest I should seem to dwell too long upon a subject neither interesting nor entertaining to my readers, I shall subjoin the following letter :—

' TO THE COOK OF THE OLLA PODRIDA.

Xanthe, retro propera.—OVID.

' MR. TARATALLA, *or whatever your name is,*

' There is at present, in this little island of Great Britain, so much hurry, bustle, and confusion, that nothing is in its proper place. O'Kelly has been taken in, the Bath butcher has been beaten, and no progress is made toward finding out the longitude. We are in the same state in which Rome was during the Catilinarian conspiracy ; no man knows upon whom he may depend ; honest men are afraid of each other ; and thieves are betrayed by their associates. The honourable fraternity of black-legs cannot follow their calling, because the management of the faro-table is in the hands of nobility : the women of fashion are at my lord mayor's dinner ; royalty is gone to a Barnet boxing-match ; and the parson of the parish lives a hundred miles from his flock, because his preferment is a sinecure.

' Not three days ago, I met my shoemaker airing himself and his household, between Hampstead and Kentish-town, in a job-coach, all dust, and sweat, and belly. The gentility of this notable tradesman's equipage induced me to make some inquiry into the state of his business and circumstances. He was candid enough to inform me (for that was his phrase, " I will candidly inform you,") that constant

* Spectator, No. 445.

attention for years to his shop had enabled him to go thus a *pleasuring* every Saturday: and, thank God, he had been able to educate his family genteelly; two daughters were then at the boarding-school at Old Brentford, and two sons at the Latin college at Knightsbridge. This honourable shoemaker's trade, being left to his journeymen, is, like the parson's, a sinecure : and he would willingly, no doubt, take the hopes of his family from the college, if he could be so fortunate as to procure him a sinecure place in the Customs; nor would it be improper, or unentertaining, to see Mrs. Last accommodated with the rangership of some forest; a genteel sinecure, like religion, charity, matrimony, honesty, and benevolence, which are become all, all sinecures !

'Mr. Last and his family are neither particular in the end they have in view, nor in the means they use to acquire that end. Yet, let them remember, that though the trouble of their shop may be carried on by proxy, and their business by those means become a sinecure, they will find ruin not to be the sinecure they willingly aim at, and that they cannot die by proxy; the former of which must as inevitably be the portion of the tradesman above his business, as the latter must of all mankind.

'The prevalent fashion seems to be, for every one to shine conspicuously, where no one expects to see him. If this total derangement of the order of things continues to spread through all ranks of people, we shall, perhaps, see the spirit of the Chevalier D'Eon, or the bruiser Ben, diffused among our fair countrywomen, or the bench of bishops huzzaing a hamstrung ox from Cripplegate to Fleet-market.

'If you call at your coachmaker's in a morning, he is trying a pair of horses for his own chariot; if in an evening, you cannot see him, for he is at the opera: your hair-dresser refuses to shave you, for he is a *ploco cosmist*, and not a barber: the barber sends his boy to do it, obliged himself to attend one of the company's dinners. A waiter will not buckle on your spurs, because it is the office of Mr. Boots, who calls his deputy; and your gentleman's gentleman, instead of pimping for his master, is intriguing for himself. If we go on at this rate, who the devil is to do the business of the world? Who will cry the pease and beans about the streets this spring? Who will sell oranges at the Abbey? Who will sweep the stage, snuff the candles, shift the scenes, make thunder and lightning, play Scrub, or dance a hornpipe? All which things are so necessary to the welfare of mankind, that without them life is a joke, and this world a vale of tears.

'Ten years hence, I shall not be surprised to find this nation so thoroughly possessed by the resolution to be all gentlemen, that house-breakers will be pardoned at the gallows, upon condition of their submitting to become pedlers, brewers, conveyancers, or lord chief-justices, for the rest of their lives; while the man who is to be transported, may, perhaps, be tempted to exchange his infamy for the drudgery of a foreign bishopric. Many an industrious handicraftsman, who has been condemned to the floating academy at Woolwich for life, will be dismissed, on pain of sitting nine years at the helm of Great Britain, giving proper security for his good behaviour. Nor will the place of master of the ceremonies at court be unprofitably filled by some well-bred lawyer from the pillory.

'Of trade and profession we shall be thus radically cured. No man can then call another apothecary! no common-councilman's heart will burst with spleen at the grandeur of a lord mayor's show: no wine-merchant need be at the trouble of committing adultery with a cargo from Portugal: no epitaph writers will be constrained to pun on the death of the cobbler: no tailor will be troubled to turn the author's breeches. *Veniet felicius ævum,* " the happier day will come," when we shall be all on a level; every man his own coachman, his own tobacconist, his own gentleman, his own man-midwife, and, as I know who would say, his own washer-woman.

I am, Mr. Taratalla, yours, &c.

Monro.   Snub.'

Nº 9. SATURDAY, MAY 12, 1787.

Mane salutantûm totis vomit ædibus undam.—Virgil.

Among the grievances of modern days, much complained of, but with little hope of redress, is the matter of receiving and paying visits, the number of which, it is generally agreed, ' has been increasing, is increased, and ought to be diminished.' You meet frequently with people, who will tell you, they are worn to death by visiting; and that, what with morning visits and afternoon visits, dining visits and supping visits, tea-drinking visits and card-playing visits, exclusive of balls and concerts, for their parts, they have not an hour to themselves in the four-and-twenty: but they must go home and dress, or they shall be too late for their visit.

Nor is this complaint by any means peculiar to the times in which we have the honour to live. Cowley was out of all patience on the subject, above a hundred years ago. ' If we engage,' says he, ' in a large acquaintance, and various familiarities, we set open our gates to the invaders of most of our time; we expose our life to a "quotidian ague of frigid impertinences," which would make a wise man tremble to think of.'

But as Cowley was apt to be a little out of humour between whiles, let us hear the honourable, pious, and sweet-tempered Mr. Boyle, who, among the troubles of life, enumerates as one ' the business of receiving senseless visits, whose continuance, if otherwise unavoidable, is capable, in my opinion, to justify the retiredness of a hermit.'

Bishop Jeremy Taylor is clear, that ' men will find it impossible to do any thing greatly good, unless they cut off all superfluous company, and visits.'

If we consult the ladies (as, indeed, we ought to do upon all occasions), we find it recorded by Ballard of the very learned and excellent Mrs. Astell, that ' when she saw needless visitors coming, whom she knew to be incapable of conversing on any useful subject, but coming merely for the sake of chat and tattle, she would look out of the window, and jestingly tell them (as Cato did Nasica), " Mrs. Astell is not at home;" and, in good earnest, kept them out, not suffering such triflers to make inroads upon her more serious hours.'

And, now, what shall we say to these things? For, after all, nothing can be more certain, than, whatever learned or unlearned folk may pretend to the contrary, visit we must, or the world will be at an end; we may as well go supercargoes to Botany-bay at once.

Distinction is the parent of perspicuity. Suppose, therefore, we take in order the different sorts of visits above mentioned, and consider them (as a worthy and valuable author phrases it) ' with their roots, reasons, and respects.'

And, first, of the first, namely, morning visits. It is evident, that, as things are now regulated amongst us, all visits of business must be made at this season; for we dine late for this very purpose; and no gentleman does any thing after dinner, but—drink. In the days of our forefathers, under Elizabeth, and her successor James, it was otherwise; for Bishop Andrews, we are told, entertained hopes of a person who had been guilty of many faults and follies, till one day the young man happened, unfortunately, to call in a morning: then the good bishop gave him up.

Mrs. Astell herself would not have disdained to take her share in a little chat and tattle over the tea-table. They may be styled correlatives, and go together as naturally as ham and chickens.

If it be asked, what number of friends it is expedient to collect, in order to make a visit comfortable, I must confess myself unable to answer the question; so diverse are the opinions and customs that have prevailed in different ages and countries. Among ourselves, at present, if one were to lay down a general rule, it should be done, perhaps, in these words: ' The more the merrier.'

Some years ago, these multitudinous meetings were known by the various names of assemblies, routs, drums, tempests, hurricanes, and earthquakes. If you made a morning visit to a lady, she would tell you, very gravely, what a divine rout, a sweet hurricane, or a charming earthquake, she had been at the night before.

To have discussed all these subdivisions of visits, and distinguished properly the nature of each, as considered in itself, would have been an arduous task, from which I find myself happily relieved, by the modern very judicious adoption of the term *party*, which is what the logicians style a *universal*, and includes every thing of the kind.

A company of twelve at dinner, with a reinforcement of eighteen at tea and cards, may, I believe, be called a *small* party, which a lady may attend, without any assistance from the hair-dresser.

There is one maxim never to be departed from; namely, that the smallness of the house is no objection to the largeness of the party : the reason is, that, as these meetings are chiefly holden in the winter, the company may keep one another warm.

But this will not, in every instance, be the case, after all the care and pains upon earth : for when the other apartments were full, I have known four persons shut into a closet, at Christmas, without fire or candle, playing a rubber by the light of a sepulchral lamp suspended from the cieling.

At another time, the butler, opening a cupboard, to take out the apparatus for the lemonade, with the nice decanters, to prevent mischief in case of weak stomachs, found two little misses, whom the lady of the house, ever anxious to promote the happiness of all her friends, had squeezed and pinioned in there, to form a snug party at cribbage.

An accident happened, last winter, at one of these amicable associations, from a contrary cause, where the fluids in the human frame had suffered too great a degree of rarefaction. A gentleman, making a precipitate retreat, on finding himself inflated, like a balloon, with a large dose of gas or burnt air in him, tumbled over a card table, which (that no room might be lost) had been set upon a landing place of the stairs. The party, with all the implements of trade, tables, cards, candles, and counters, and the unfortunate person who had brought on the catastrophe, rolled down together. No farther mischief, however, was done ; and two gentlemen of the party, as I have been well informed, found time to make a bet on the *odd trick*, before they got to the bottom.

But these are trifling circumstances, and no more than may be expected to fall to the lot of humanity.

I do not mention them, I am sure, as constituting any objection to a *party*, or as affording any reason why one should deprive *one's* self of the pleasure *one* always has in *seeing one's friends about one.*—Z.

BISHOP HORNE.

After the remarks of my kind and ingenious correspondent Z, the lucubrations of Mr. Taratalla, will, I fear, afford little entertainment; however,

> Edita ne brevibus pereat mea charta libellis,
> Dicatur potius τον δ' απαμειβομενος.—MARTIAL.

> Rather than leave my page half fill'd, I'd scrawl,
> ' A cobbler there was, and he lived in his stall.'

All periodical writers, are, by their profession and place, censors of the public manners; and that their office may be discharged with fidelity and skill, they should possess a certain degree of that virtù and connoisseurship which pervades all things, from the tying of a cravat, to the demonstration of the *pons asininus*. They claim a right to be believed in every thing they may advance; to be admired for that ingenuity which they undoubtedly possess; and to be patronised and encouraged by the discerning many. Should they sometimes relate adventures they may have met with in a stage-coach, in the lobby of a playhouse, or among the triflers of the drawing-room; their readers are bound in honour to believe that they have not, all their life long, been actuated by that high-minded spirit which usually excites authors to mount the top of a coach, to soar into the twelve-penny gallery, and to leave the splendour of the drawing-room to ' low ambition and the pride of kings.'

Unfortunately for myself and my readers, I do not unite in my own person all those qualifications which should adorn a professor of painting, dancing, music,

F 3

electricity, horsemanship, and half a score more
things of the same nature, all of which, in the course
of my business, I shall be expected to deal out to
my customers. In order to supply those deficiencies
in myself, which I sincerely lament, I have settled a
regular correspondence with some honest gentlemen
of the quill, of great credit, and great stock-in-trade,
from whose kind assistance I hope to give universal
satisfaction. When I first hinted my proposal to the
literati, mentioning the terms upon which I purposed
employing any two or three hands who might be out
of work, I received, among others, the following answer to my advertisement.

' TO THE AUTHOR OF THE OLLA PODRIDA.

  ' SIR,
  ' I am an excellent scholar, a man of great abilities,
extensive knowledge, and of infinite wit and humour.
I have written twelve essays, which will do very great
honour to, and very much increase the reputation of
your work ; all which I will let you have for half-a-
guinea, and will throw you half a score epigrams into
the bargain. I would have waited upon you myself
with them ; but, Sir, my shirt is washing, and my coat
is gone to be mended.   I am, Sir,
          Your most obedient humble servant,
                              JOHN SCRIBE.'

I hastened to Mr. Scribe's lodgings, at Paddington.—I shall not here give a very minute description
of the different modes of salutation with which two
authors come together, lest some of my readers, who
are disposed to turn the gravest things into ridicule,
should be inclined to laugh, particularly as my friend
before observed, that his shirt was with his laundress
and his coat with the tailor. Suffice it therefore to

say, that, after a mutual interchange of compliments, he celebrating my liberality, and I his talents, we proceeded to discuss the business which had occasioned our meeting. The engagement entered into between us was soon concluded upon, and produced a confidential intimacy, which excited Mr. Scribe to favour me with some insight into his own character, opinions, and adventures. But as in the ardour of a new-formed friendship I promised to give his complete life to the world, in two volumes octavo, price fourteen shillings, to be sold by all the booksellers in town and country, I will not anticipate the pleasure my readers will have in the perusal of my work, by mutilated and imperfect sketches of that history, which will soon be presented to them whole and uncorrupt.

Upon taking leave of my Paddington friend, as he followed me down stairs, he very obligingly offered his assistance in the framing of any advertisements which might be necessary or conducive to the sale of my work. He then shewed me, as specimens of his talents in this species of writing, an essay on leather breeches, made upon mathematical principles, and a recommendation of the concave razor. These, he observed, were works of a lighter kind, and such as he called επεα ποικιλα, *or the amusements of Paddington.* I thanked him, but declined the acceptance of his offer.

Upon my return home, I found three or four visitants had called upon business similar to Mr. Scribe's: amongst whom an Hibernian stay-maker, from the Borough, wished to enlist in my service, and in testimony of his abilities, had left a parcel of dreams of his own composing, which are ushered in by complaints of his inability to sleep. A French marquis, to whom the air of Great Britain had been recommended by his physicians, left word, that, having nothing else to do, he had condescended, during his residence in this island, purely from his *penchant* for the science, and *pour passer le temps,* to instruct the noblesse in dancing. This course of life, he very properly observed, gave him many opportunities of furnishing me with intelligence from the beau monde ; and accordingly my readers will frequently see how things go on from the authentic information of the marquis.

MONRO.—*Scribe's Letter by* LEYCESTER.

<hr>

Nº 10.   SATURDAY, MAY 19, 1787.

Vivite felices, quibus est fortuna peracta
Jam sua.—— VIRGIL.

IN expatiating upon the transient brevity of all sublunary happiness, moralists of every age and climate have shewn themselves desirous of indulging in the flights of their imaginations. Human life has been severally compared to a race, to the gliding course of a river, to a moveable procession, and to many other fleeting appearances, of which each part exists by the cessation or non-commencement of existence in the rest. It is upon the same principles that, by philosophers of more abstruse speculation, time, from its successive continuity, has been demonstrated never to be present. To make the proper use then of these demonstrations, one might easily prove the absurdity of reposing our happiness upon present time which has been allowed to have no existence, and of attempting to build a real superstructure upon the imaginary basis of a nonentity. But if our felicity cannot originate from sensation or the enjoyment of the present moment, it must of course be derived either from a speculative anticipation of futurity, or a soothing remembrance of pleasures already enjoyed. To contrast then these two original sources, shall be the subject of the following paper, that we may be enabled to discriminate which of the two is more desirable, from the permanency of those pleasures it bestows, and their independency of external support.

In the contemplation of future life, our thoughts must of necessity be agitated by the most powerful passions inherent in our frame. Hope and Fear, which have always been found to have most influence upon human actions, are the passions which give a tincture of themselves to all our views, whilst we look forward into futurity. If the prospect before us appear cheerful and serene, Hope communicates to us a pleasure as lively in the view of it, as Sensation could in the enjoyment; and though a disappointment of our expectations may deprive us of this imaginary bliss, and convince us of the error which we have been cherishing in our bosoms; yet it is that kind of error *(mentis gratissimus)* from which it gives us real pain to be separated. On the contrary, whatever good fortune may await us, if we have no reason to flatter ourselves with the expectation of it; if, as far as human eye can penetrate, the prospect before us appear a dark and dreary waste, the fear of incumbent misfortunes renders our sufferings more painful, than if we actually laboured under the evils which we only apprehend, and sinks us in all the ' misery of fancied woe.'

We see then, that in the anticipation of life we frequently make ourselves miserable by the apprehension of evils which we never experience; and that the pleasures which are derived from Hope,

though acute and brilliant, are neither permanent,
nor independent of external support. Their duration, indeed, must inevitably be destroyed by the
revolution of time, which brings with it the object
that we have in view : and if our hopes then prove
to have been ill-grounded, the chagrin of frustrated
expectations is a consequence too obvious to need
being mentioned : but if we are even fortunate
enough to meet with a full completion of our wishes,
it does not equally follow, that we should enjoy the
happiness proposed : perhaps, after all, we shall
find a kind of disappointment even in the gratification of our desires ; for appearances of happiness
fill the eye with fancied grandeur at a distance, but,
contrary to other objects of sight, gradually diminish
upon the nearness of our approach. But the idea
of felicity being derived from hope, will appear still
more groundless if we consider the uncertainty which
must necessarily attend it. When we rely upon
events which are yet to come, we submit ourselves
to the direction of an arbitrary and capricious fortune; and shall, perhaps, to our misfortune experience, that the best concerted schemes, and most
probable expectations, are easily frustrated by innumerable casualties, which it is not in our power
to foresee, nor, if we foresee, to prevent. It is not,
however, requisite to enlarge upon that most trite of
all topics, the instability of human events ; enough,
I think, has been said to prove, that whatever bliss
we may propose to ourselves in contemplating the
bright appearances of our future life, and ' in fancy
swallowing up the space between,' it cannot possibly be either permanent or self-derived ; which
qualities, though they be not of themselves able to
form a complete system of happiness, are yet so far
necessary, as to render any system incomplete which
is without them.

I shall now take a view of those pleasures which arise from a retrospect of our past lives, and endeavour so to contrast them with those already considered, as may make them appear with additional beauty from the comparison.

It must, however, be allowed that, situated as we are in this world, subservient to the smiles and frowns of fortune, a serene tranquillity is the highest happiness we have reason to expect, and that the subtle pleasure, which is pursued with so much avidity by the gay and the dissipated, is a mere phantom, without any other existence than in the imaginations of its eager votaries. Hence the pleasures which originate from a cool and dispassionate use of our reason must be more satisfactory than those which we derive from the violent emotions of our most forcible passions. But in no exercise can we employ our reasoning faculty to greater advantage, than when we conjecture with superior certainty upon future events, by well considering and reflecting upon those which we have already experienced.

We have before seen that in our views of futurity, we are liable to be made miserable by the dread of bad fortune, as well as happy by the sanguine preoccupation of good. Here then the pleasures of reflection evidently prove themselves superior; for the review of past happiness does not convey to us any higher satisfaction than the remembrance of difficulties which we have surmounted. It is here, at last, that, freed from the shackles of fortune, and every other external power which may have before entangled us, we make all our happiness centre within ourselves; and, like the industrious bees that produce honey as well out of bitter herbs as sweet, even out of the evils of life we extract the choicest and most refined bliss. Indeed, in the midst of our misfortunes we may be consoled by the consideration of being at some future period entertained with the thoughts of what now gives us pain; as Æneas is represented supporting his dejected companions by a similar consolation:

Forsan et hæc olim meminisse juvabit.—VIRG.

And as this bliss is self-derived and independent of any thing external, so is it also durable; for, as it is drawn from those transactions which we are conscious have already taken place, it is evident that nothing can put a period to its existence but the annihilation of that consciousness and faculty of remembering whence it was originally derived. From this consideration, it is plain, that a life of activity and exertion is so much the more preferable to a life of indolence and repose, as it affords more room for the exercise of this faculty. Our happiness, we have before seen, arises from the recollection of past pleasures, proportionably chequered with the remembrance of hardships which we have surmounted. Now the engagements of society so intersperse an active live with the anxious vicissitudes of hope and fear, that we must unavoidably meet with many difficulties unknown in the still path of retirement, which, though disagreeable when encountered, nevertheless convey a secret satisfaction to the mind in reflecting on them when subdued. The man, indeed, who secludes himself from the cares of the world, remains at the same time unroused by the pleasing emotions which others enjoy; and in the decline of age will look back upon the continued sameness of his past life with a listless indifference; for if in the sunshine of youth his happiness glow with a warmth scarcely vital, how can the remembrance of it as faintly reflected by a lukewarm imagination cheer his drooping spi-

rits in the winter of old age? In opposition to this
languor of a life worn out in inaction, it may, perhaps, be needless to instance with what lively spirits
the aged votaries of ambition or wealth indulge
themselves in ease after the toils of a long and
laborious pursuit after their respective objects;
with what pleasure the soldier dwells upon the
narrative of his honourable though dangerous exploits, how the sailor rejoices whilst he recounts the
rocks and tempests which he has so perilously surmounted.

——Gaudent ut vertice raso
Garrula securi narrare pericula nautæ.—Juv.

But as all human happiness must inevitably be al-
loyed by some mixture of evil, and as the above view
of the pleasure of reflection may seem to imply a
species of happiness more perfect than is consistent
with our present state, after having seen the joys
which attend it, let us now examine into its concomitant evils; let us consider whether the debau-
chee, when the decay of his faculties prompts him
to indulge in an indolent repose, looks back with solid satisfaction upon those vicissitudes of pleasure
and pain, the former of which he is conscious of
having purchased at the expense of his innocence,
the latter of having merited by his guilt; whether
the remorse, arising from the consciousness of having violated every principle of justice and generosity, be compensated to the miser, by considering
with what labour he has amassed his accumulated
hoards: and, if upon this inquiry we find that the
review of his past conduct serves rather to increase
than to alleviate his present pains, we shall be led
to infer, that the testimony of a good conscience is
another requisite towards completing that happiness
which we have in view. He, who by his worldly
wisdom is enabled to withstand the most violent at-

XLI.   G

tacks of fortune, if he possess not this cheerful companion within his breast, will still be a stranger to any true peace or comfort; he will view even the smiles of prosperity without satisfaction, and, finding nought but a turbulent confusion in his own bosom, will shrink back with horror from himself. It appears then, that though many accidental circumstances may contribute to heighten the beauties of this review, the essential requisite is a mind conscious of unerring rectitude; and, as this is entirely dependant upon ourselves, that we have it in our power, by our own conduct, to provide for the decline of age, when our natural infirmities require an additional consolation, a never-failing source of true and placid enjoyment.

I have seen it somewhere recommended, that, in order to enjoy the pleasures of the imagination in our nightly dreams, we should be able to rest upon our pillow, and reflect coolly upon the transactions of the preceding day. In the same manner I should recommend it to every one so to regulate his conduct through the active scenes of social life, that he may lie down in the evening of old age, and review them with unruffled satisfaction; and, as we have observed that the happiness derived from hope, though inferior to that of reflection, is not however trivial, I would also recommend him so to extract and mingle the joys of each, as to make the soothing remembrance of past pleasures a solid foundation for a speculative anticipation of those to come.

ANON.

Nº 11. SATURDAY, MAY 26, 1787.

Smiles from reason flow, to brutes denied.—Milton.

It has been the business of philosophers in all ages to invent an apposite and characteristic term by which man may be distinguished from the brute creation in his exclusive right to some peculiar faculty. The deep penetration and vigorous researches of an illustrious heathen have enabled him to inform us, that man is an *animal bipes implume*, a two-legged animal without feathers. And philosophers of later ages have discovered, that he is a laughing animal, a rational animal, a tool-making animal, a cooking animal.

It is my present intention to consider him as the laughing animal; and that faculty, though it should resolve itself into as many subdivisions as a lecture upon heads, or branch forth into ramifications like a Welsh pedigree, I shall pursue through all its degrees, from the *risus sardonicus* of the ancients, to the *tee-hee* of the modern drawing-room.

When I insist upon the gravity of the subject I am about to handle, lest I should be accused of extravagance of opinion, I shall endeavour to shew, by a brief narrative of facts, that the consequences which flow from the use and abuse of this our distinguishing faculty are of the most serious nature. I have seen a whole battalion of militia men, as valorous and as red-coated as a regiment of guards, disconcerted and put into confusion in the midst of their manœuvring and tobacco-chewing, from the broad-shouldered serjeant of the grenadier company, to the duck-legged corporal of recruits, by the horse-laugh of a by-stander. I was once present (*credite dicenti*) in the pit at the Opera, during the representation of Macbeth; on my right hand sat an unthinking Englishman, who, forgetful that he was a spectator of a serious performance, burst into a horse-laugh, just at the very time when Lady Macbeth and her *caro sposo* were conjuring up all the horror that heads and heels were capable of exciting. Her ladyship, conscious that she brandished her dagger in tune, and that she rubbed off the ' damn'd spot' from her hand most harmoniously, without exhibiting to the audience any of that *disagreeabilità* of countenance for which Mrs. Siddons has been condemned, was very highly as well as very justly enraged. The curtain fell, and the signora declared she would never appear again before an English audience. In vain did the distressed manager represent to her, that the taste, the judgment, the very every thing of this unhappy nation, were infinitely beneath her notice; heaping at the same time upon poor John Bull a profusion of epithets, all ending in *issimo*. In vain was he pressing in his solicitations, that she should give them, at least, one more trial: she still persisted in her cruel threats, that she would leave them, and return to her own country. At last, however, the kind interference of a noble frequenter of the opera-house produced a reconciliation. He could not but confess the headstrong vulgarity and unreasonable prejudices of his countrymen, who considered every competition with their favourite poet as a burlesque and an insult: yet, he hoped, the ignorance and the insolence of a few would not be a sufficient reason for the punishment of the great body of *cognoscenti*. He moreover spiritedly declared, that he would call any person to a very severe account, who should dare to laugh, when on the printed bills of the night was written, in large characters, ' a serious opera.'

The resentment of Signor Macabet himself was carried to a still higher pitch. He who but the day before had been complimented with the thaneship of Cawdor, because he had stood a minute and a half longer, by the manager's watch, upon one leg, than any Macbeth or Artaxerxes who had ever appeared upon any stage, was actually found the next morning hanging in a pair of embroidered garters, with tassels of silver twist. The signor made a vacancy in the opera list, and his garters were entirely spoiled, having been so much stretched as to be unfit for the use of any future Macbeth, Rinaldo Artaxerxes, or, in short, any body with a decent leg.

This tragical after-piece was entirely occasioned by the horse-laugh, the use of which is sometimes allowable, but the too frequent repetition of it I cannot but consider as a disease. This disease is very prevalent in the city; it is often found at a sitting of the quorum, and, in short, at most places where the company meet to be merry: the symptoms attending it are violent convulsions, and a bloated habit.

This disorder, among the men, I believe to have originated from the false philosophy of a few smatterers in science, who conceived, that as man was distinguished from the brutes by laughter, the more he laughed the farther he was removed from the lower species. Yet they should, in their philosophical researches, have recollected, that extremes meet, and for that very reason this species of laughter, which being too much indulged, was considered as unbecoming mankind, has been degraded by the title of the *horse-laugh*. With the ladies, this complaint has a different origin. The Venus of the Greeks, from whom we derive all our notions of the elegant and beautiful, when represented by the poets in her most bewitching attire, is called the

φιλομειδης, a term expressive of that rational cheerfulness of countenance, which comprehends all that
is lovely in the female face. The poverty of our
language has been obliged to translate this ' the
laughter-loving:' and to that cause alone are owing
all those shrill, yet violent sallies of misinterpreted
gaiety, which frighten our horses in the Park, give
us the head-ache at old Drury, and, worse than
all, distort the features of the fairest women in the
world.

Of grinning, which I do not consider as a species
of laughter, I shall treat upon some future occasion,
and endeavour to describe the different modifica-
tions of it, as it is at present practised by those professors who exercise their faculty through a horse-
collar, at a country fair, by that useful animal in the
kitchen, the turnspit, and by the illustrious assistant
and partner of Mr. Astley, general Jackoo.

I shall proceed, therefore, to the *risus in angulo*
of the ladies, or giggle in the corner. This species
of merriment has many different ends in view. It
sometimes hunts down a man of bashfulness, sometimes ridicules a hump-back or a red nose, and
sometimes becomes an assignation of gallantry. The
two former of its qualities are particularly called
forth, when a bevy of beauties, huddled up into one
corner of a room, monopolize the wit of a whole company, and exercise all the cruel artillery of stolen
glances and half-stifled laughs, to the great disquiet
of any man who is not as serene amidst difficulties as Fabricius was in the tent of King Pyrrhus.

That the giggle in the corner is sometimes an assignation of gallantry, my male readers, who have
no authority upon which they can with more confidence rely, will find sufficiently demonstrated in
Horace. My female readers are reminded of a
manœuvre of this kind, by some lines in the first

pastoral of Mr. Pope. He there makes a shepherd give the following account, which by-the-by I think hardly fair:

> Me gentle Delia beckons from the plain,
> Then, hid in shades, eludes her eager swain;
> But feigns a laugh, to see me search around,
> And by that laugh the willing fair is found.

The *tee-hee* is that gentle relaxation of the muscular system which proceeds from no inward impulse, and is vulgarly, though not improperly, denoted the affected laugh. This is a term of great latitude, and comprehends the laugh of all those who are called, by the Guardian,* the Chians, the Ionics, and the Megarics. The *tee-hee* is the tribute generally paid to any story which is supposed to be a witty one, but not perfectly understood; it is the chorus of a scandalizing tea-table, the condescension of a great man, and the pride of a little one; the resource of dulness, and the ornament of a good set of teeth.

To discover the origin of this, I have toiled through all the chronological books I could think of, but to no purpose. However, from the oral tradition of an old weather-wise gentleman, who is accustomed to note remarkable occurrences, I learn that it came into this country with Lord Chesterfield, upon his return from his travels. It was at first confined entirely to his lordship's suite; it then diffused itself, by degrees, through St. James's and its environs; and last of all became the common property of those who were distinguished by the appellation of good company. Still, however, the practice of tee-heeing was far from general; citizens were unacquainted with it, for my lady mayoress had no routs; and though it once rode to Rumford with a

* Number 29.

gentleman out of livery, and was there dropped, yet, as no one understood it, no one thought proper to pick it up. The happy improvement of our manners has now made that science universal, which for a long time was partial; good company, refinement, and tee-heeing, are now as common and as cheap as hack-parsons, or Welsh mutton; we may dine with them at a shilling ordinary on Sundays; are overrun with them at a masquerade; elbowed to death by them in the little hell at Newmarket; lose our handkerchiefs to them in the lobby of the playhouse; and get trampled under their feet at a bull-baiting in Moorfields. About five weeks ago I fell in with a tee-heeing highwayman in Epping Forest. He was too accomplished and too well mounted for me to think of keeping such company long; and we parted, after I had deposited with him five pennyworth of halfpence, a metal watch-chain, and an ode to the spring, which, after some trouble, I convinced him was as good as the Bank.

After all that can be said on this subject, we may as well think of separating wit from the first of April, or goose from Michaelmas-day, as that we can live at ease without laughter, 'the chorus of conversation,' and the union of social intercourse.

The raptures of poetic imagination have extended this faculty to every part of the creation, in a strain of metaphorical allusion, adopted by all poets, in all ages and countries: in Milton we find,

—— all things *smiled*
With fragrance, and with joy my heart o'erflow'd.

And in that higher species of poetry, it is said of the valleys, they shall stand so thick with corn, that they shall *laugh* and sing.

It is not then the thing itself of which we can complain, but the abuse and mismanagement of it.

He is no object of imitation or envy, who can morosely withhold his laughter, when he may indulge it, without incurring the charge of folly; nor is that man much to be esteemed, who, with ignorance, affectation, arrogance, and ill-nature, usurps the privilege of laughing upon all occasions, without regard to situation, circumstance, or decorum.

MONRO.

Nº 12. SATURDAY, JUNE 2, 1787.

I MADE an entrance, in a former paper, on the important subject of visiting, and distinguishing the different kinds of visits now in vogue amongst us, with their excellences and defects.

It is hard, indeed, to guess at the pleasure of assembling in very large parties. There is much heat, hurry, and fatigue, to all who are concerned. The essence of the entertainment seems to consist in a crowd, and none appear to be perfectly happy while they can stir hand or foot. At least, this is the case with the lady of the house, whose supreme felicity it is, to be kept *in equilibrio*, by an equilateral pressure from all quarters. Fixed in her orb, like the sun of the system, she dispenses the favour of her nods and smiles on those bodies, which—I wish I could say—*move* around her; but that they cannot do.

But though pleasure be not obtained, trouble perhaps, it may be said, is saved, by receiving a multitude at once, instead of being subject to their perpetual incursions in separate bodies; and when the polite mob has been at my house, I am at rest for some time. True: but then there is a reciprocity:

and as others have assisted in making your mob a decent and respectable one, you must do the same by them, and every evening will pass in this *rondeau of delights*; a vortex, out of which none can emerge, and into which more and more are continually drawn, for fear of being left in solitude; as all who wish to visit will very soon be obliged to visit after this method, or not at all. From the metropolis the fashion has made its way into provincial towns, all the visitable inhabitants of which will be assembled together at one house or other, through the winter; and this, though perhaps there is not a single person among them, who does not dislike and complain of the custom, as absurd and disagreeable.

For the conduct of these visits no directions can be laid down; but concerning others (while any such shall remain) where a moderate company of neighbours meet, to pass a little time in conversation, some observations may be offered.

They are useful and indeed necessary, to maintain a friendly and social intercourse, without which we are not in a capacity to give or receive help and assistance from each other.

They are useful to cheer and refresh the spirits after business, and may render us fitter to return to it again.

They are useful, when they are made with a view of relieving and comforting such as are afflicted and distressed; and that, not only in great and signal troubles, but the common cares and concerns of life; of advising exhorting, and consoling such as, having weak and low spirits, are oppressed by anxiety and melancholy; of which in England the number always has been, and always will be, very considerable. Time is well employed in these and the like good offices, where a friend is the best physician. The very sight of a cheerful friend is often like the sun breaking forth in a cloudy day. A melancholy person is at least as much the object of charity as a sick one. The cheerful owe this duty to those who are otherwise; and enjoy, themselves, the most refined and exalted kind of pleasure, when they find their endeavours to succeed.

Visits are useful, when they become the means of acquiring or communicating useful knowledge, relative to the conduct of life, in concerns either personal or domestic; or, even when no such knowledge is obtained, if by innocent mirth, pleasant tales, &c. people are brought into good humour, and kept in it. No recreation is more truly serviceable and effectual than this : and it is said of Archbishop Williams, that, ' the greater the performance he was about to undertake (whether a speech, a sermon, or a debate), the more liberty and recreation he first took, to quicken and open his spirits, and to clear his thoughts.'

By visiting, opportunities are offered of introducing occasionally matters literary and religious, new publications, &c. For though, perhaps, this is not so often done as it might be, when people meet; yet it cannot be done at all, unless people do meet.

To render visits lively and agreeable, where the company is small, and it can be managed conveniently, the conversation should be general. The ladies, by their sprightliness, should animate the gentlemen, and the gentlemen, by their learning, inform the ladies. Instead of this, the gentlemen too often lay their heads together, on one side of the room, and talk on subjects of literature or politics; leaving the ladies to settle the articles of caps and gowns, blonds and gauzes, on the other; which is hardly fair, especially in these days, when so many of the other sex are qualified to join in a conversation on more important topics.

The end of a visit is frustrated, if it be made too long; as when the same company sit together from three in the afternoon till twelve at night, or nine hours; for then, that which was designed for a recreation becomes itself a burden, unless there be some particular business or amusement in hand.

Live not in a perpetual round and hurry of visiting. You will neglect your affairs at home; you will by degrees contract a dislike to home, and a dread of being alone; than which nothing can be more wretched and pernicious. You will acquire a habit of being idle, of gossiping, dealing in slander, scandal, &c. and of inducing others to do the same.

In a small party, as also in a single family, the work-basket and a book agree well together. While the ladies work, let one person read distinctly and deliberately, making proper pauses for remarks and observations; these will furnish conversation for a while; when it begins to flag, let the reader go on, till fresh matter supplies fresh conversation. A winter evening passes pleasantly in this manner; and a general wish will be expressed, that it had been longer. The mind becomes stored with knowledge, and the tongue accustomed to speak upon profitable subjects.

Rousseau asserts, that every person in a company should have something to do. I see not how this can well be contrived; but his reason is curious, and deserves consideration. ' In my opinion,' says he, ' idleness is no less the pest of society, than of solitude. Nothing contracts the mind, nothing engenders trifles, tales, backbiting, slander, and falsities, so much as being shut up in a room, opposite each other, and reduced to no other occupation than the necessity of continual chattering. When all are employed, they speak only when they have something to say; but if you are doing nothing, you must absolutely talk incessantly, which of all constraints is the most troublesome and the most dangerous. I dare go even farther, and maintain, that to render a circle truly agreeable, every one must be not only doing something, but something which requires a little attention.'

Should this plan of Rousseau be favourably received, and a notion be entertained of carrying it into execution, the chief difficulty will be to provide proper employment for the gentlemen. My readers will turn the matter in their minds. The only case in point, which I can recollect of at present, is that of a friend, who, when young, amused himself with making partridge-nets. On a visit, he would take his work out of the bag, hitch one end of the net upon a sconce, and proceed to business. His example militates powerfully in favour of the plan; for his conversation, while so employed, was remarkably free and easy.

Under the above regulations, we can never be the worse, and, if we keep tolerable company, shall generally be the better, for a visit. Something must occur, which is worth remembering and noting down. A reflection at the end of a visit will soon shew, whether it comes properly under the denomination of those condemned by casuists, as useless and impertinent; since that is useless which tends to no good purpose; and that is impertinent, which claims your time and attention, and gives nothing in return.

Z.   Bishop Horne.

Nº 13. SATURDAY, JUNE 9, 1787.

WHEN a friend told Johnson that he was much blamed for having unveiled the weakness of Pope, ' Sir,' said he, ' if one man undertake to write the life of another, he undertakes to exhibit his true and real character : but this can be done only by a faithful and accurate delineation of the particulars which discriminate that character.'

The biographers of this great man seem conscientiously to have followed the rule thus laid down by him, and have very fairly communicated all they knew, whether to his advantage or otherwise. Much concern, disquietude, and offence, have been occasioned by this their conduct in the minds of many, who apprehend, that the cause in which he stood forth will suffer by the infirmities of the advocate being thus exposed to the prying and malignant eye of the world.

But did these persons then ever suppose, or did they imagine that the world ever supposed, Dr. Johnson to have been a perfect character ? Alas! no : we all know how that matter stands, if we ever look into our own hearts, and duly watch the current of our own thoughts, words, and actions. Johnson was honest, and kept a faithful diary of these, which is before the public. Let any man do the same for a fortnight, and publish it : and if, after that, he should find himself so disposed, let him ' cast a stone.' At that hour when the failings of all shall be made manifest, the attention of each individual will be confined to his own.

It is not merely the name of Johnson that is to do service to any cause. It is his genius, his learning, his good sense, the strength of his reasonings, and the happiness of his illustrations. These all are precisely what they were: once good, and always good. His arguments in favour of self-denial do not lose their force, because he fasted; nor those in favour of devotion, because he said his prayers. Grant his failings were, if possible, still greater than these: will a man refuse to be guided by the sound opinion of a counsel, or resist the salutary prescription of a physician, because they who give them are not without their faults? A man may do so; but he will never be accounted a wise man for doing it.

Johnson, it is said, was superstitious. But who shall exactly ascertain to us what superstition is? The Romanist is charged with it by the church-of-England man; the churchman by the presbyterian; the presbyterian by the independent; all by the deist; and the deist by the atheist. With some it is superstition to pray, with others to receive the sacrament, with others to believe in revelation, with others to believe in God. In some minds it springs from the most amiable disposition in the world—' a pious awe, and fear to have offended;' a wish rather to do too much than too little Such a disposition one loves and wishes always to find in a friend; and it cannot be disagreeable in the sight of him who made us: it argues a sensibility of heart, a tenderness of conscience, and the fear of God. Let him, who finds it not in himself, beware lest, in flying from superstition, he fall into irreligion and profaneness.

That persons of eminent talents and attainments in literature have been often complained of as— dogmatical, boisterous, and inattentive to the rules of good breeding, is well known. But let us not expect every thing from every man. There was no occasion that Johnson should teach us to dance, to make bows, or turn compliments. He could teach us better things. To reject wisdom, because the person of him who communicates it is uncouth, and his manners are inelegant—what is it, but to throw away a pine-apple, and assign for a reason the roughness of its coat? Who quarrels with a botanist for not being an astronomer, or with a moralist for not being a mathematician? As it is said in concerns of a much higher nature, 'every man hath his gift, one after this manner, and another after that;' it is our business to profit by all, and to learn of each that in which each is best qualified to instruct us.

That Johnson was generous and charitable, none can deny. But he was not always judicious in the selection of his objects; distress was a sufficient recommendation, and he did not scrutinize into the failings of the distressed. May it be always my lot to have such a benefactor! Some are so nice in a scrutiny of this kind, that they can never find any proper objects of their benevolence, and are necessitated to save their money. It should doubtless be distributed in the best manner we are able to distribute it; but what would become of us all, if he, on whose bounty all depend, should be ' extreme to mark that which is done amiss?'

It is hard to judge any man, without a due consideration of all circumstances. Here were stupendous abilities, and suitable attainments; but then here were hereditary disorders of body and mind reciprocally aggravating each other; a scrofulous frame, and a melancholy temper; here was a life, the greater part of which passed in making provision for the day, under the pressure of poverty and sickness, sorrow and anguish. So far to gain the ascendant over these, as to do what Johnson did, required very great strength of mind indeed. Who can say, that, in a like situation, he should long have possessed, or been able to exert it?

From the mixture of power and weakness in the composition of this wonderful man, the scholar should learn humility. It was designed to correct that pride which great parts and great learning are apt to produce in their possessor. In him it had the desired effect. For though consciousness of superiority might sometimes induce him to carry it high with man (and even this was much abated in the latter part of life), his devotions have shewn to the whole world, how humbly he walked at all times with his God.

His example may likewise encourage those of timid and gloomy dispositions not to despond, when they reflect, that the vigour of such an intellect could not preserve its possessor from the depredations of melancholy. They will cease to be surprised and alarmed at the degree of their own sufferings: they will resolve to bear, with patience and resignation, the malady to which they find a Johnson subject, as well as themselves: and if they want words, in which to ask relief from him who alone can give it, the God of mercy, and Father of all comfort, language affords no finer than those in which his prayers are conceived. Child of sorrow, whoever thou art, use them; and be thankful, that the man existed, by whose means thou hast them to use.

His eminence and his fame must of course have excited envy and malice: but let envy and malice look at his infirmities and his charities, and they will quickly melt into pity and love.

That he should not be conscious of the abilities with which Providence had blessed him, was impossible. He felt his own powers; he felt what he was

capable of having performed; and he saw how little, comparatively speaking, he had performed.
Hence his apprehensions on the near prospect of the
account to be made, viewed through the medium of
constitutional and morbid melancholy, which often
excluded from his sight the bright beams of divine
mercy. May those beams ever shine upon us! But
let them not cause us to forget, that talents have
been bestowed, of which an account must be rendered; and that the fate of the ' unprofitable servant' may justly beget apprehensions in the stoutest
mind. The indolent man, who is without such apprehensions, has never yet considered the subject as
he ought. For one person who fears death too much,
there are a thousand who do not fear it enough, nor
have thought in earnest about it. Let us only put
in practice the duty of self-examination; let us inquire into the success we have experienced in our
war against the passions, or even against undue indulgence of the common appetites, eating, drinking,
and sleeping; we shall soon perceive how much
more easy it is to form resolutions, than to execute
them; and shall no longer find occasion, perhaps,
to wonder at the weakness of Johnson.

On the whole—In the memoirs of him that have
been published, there are so many witty sayings,
and so many wise ones, by which the world, if it so
please, may be at once entertained and improved,
that I do not regret their publication. In this, as in
all other instances, we are to adopt the good and reject the evil. The little stories of his oddities and
his infirmities in common life will, after a while, be
overlooked and forgotten; but his writings will live
for ever, still more and more studied and admired,
while Britons shall continue to be characterized by
a love of elegance and sublimity, of good sense and
virtue. The sincerity of his repentance, the stead-

fastness of his faith, and the fervour of his charity, forbid us to doubt that his sun set in clouds, to rise without them: and of this let us always be mindful, that every one who is made better by his books, will add a wreath to his crown.—Z.

BISHOP HORNE.

Nᵒ 14. SATURDAY, JUNE 16, 1787.

BETWEEN the sloven and the coxcomb there is generally a competition which shall be the more contemptible, the one in the total neglect of every thing which might make his appearance in public supportable; and the other in the cultivation of every superfluous ornament. The former offends by his negligence and dirt, the latter by his airs and perfumery. Each entertains a proper contempt for the other; and while both are right in their opinion, both are wrong in their practice. The dress of a man is almost invariably an indication of his habit of mind: I do not mean to assert, that by a red coat you can positively swear to his valour, or by a black one to his integrity; but from his general manner of adorning his person, you may discover the general train of his thinking. He who has never been seen in dishabille but by his hair-dresser or his valet-de-chambre, I am inclined to suppose has never known the luxury of mental relaxation. Not that his mind is occupied in abstruse speculations; but, being ever solicitous for the welfare and ornament of his person, he cannot descend to take a share in those concerns of the world, which, if they gained possession of his mind, might discompose the features of his face. He has no consolation for the afflicted,* for care produceth wrinkles; he shuns laughter, lest he should shake the powder from his curls; he cannot smoke lest his coat should smell of tobacco; and he is prevented from the moderate use of wine, for it would endanger, if not ruin, his complexion.

These well-dressed advocates for virtue avoid gluttony, not that they may practise abstinence, but lest they should injure their shapes; they fly from drunkenness, not because it is a vice, dangerous in itself and destructive in its consequences, but that they may preserve their faces from pimples. Reasons of equal moment regulate all their actions, concerns, and opinions. The man of dress is, perchance, a dissenter, because the pathway which leads to the meeting-house is cleaner than that to the church; or he is a churchman, because his pew is lined with green baize.

There is an equivocal species of beings, called *petites maitres*, who are owned by neither sex, and shunned by both. They are a race not peculiar to any nation,† or clime, or country. Ancient Rome had many of them; Modern Rome, has, I suspect, more. They flourish among our pacified friends in France; nor are we in England entirely without them. We may soon, perhaps, hear of their exist-

---

* He is one of that uncomfortable species so happily delineated in the learned preface to Bellendenus:

Ψυχραν εχει παις καρδιαν ϑερμοις επι·
Υδαρες τε πως, και λεπτον αιμ' αει τρεφων·
Νηφειν τ' απιστειν τ' αρθρα του βιου λεγει,
Αοινον, αγελαστον, απροσπηγορου τερας.

† They are evidently alluded to in the following epigram of Ausonius:

Dum dubitat natura marem faceretne puellam,
Factus es, O pulcher, pæne puella, puer!

ence among our colonists at Botany-bay ; that they have sprung up in the fashionable part of Lapland, or are gaining ground with the paper money in North America.

To this part of the creation is almost entirely confined that violent extravagance of dress which fixes a man's head between two capes or promontories, like an attorney in the pillory, and cuts away the skirts of his coat, as if he had narrowly escaped from a fire. Among these whimsical innovators in dress, I have found all my conclusions respecting the state of their minds built upon unsound foundations. The same spirit of innovation, which was continually varying the position of the sleeve-button, or the pattern of the stocking, might, I thought, render them unquiet members of the community, and dangerous to the state. But I am happily mistaken. They are harmless citizens ; and those minds which, in my patriotic zeal, I was too fearful might be plotting against my country, I have, upon a closer examination, discovered to be a perfect blank.

Somewhat of a man's mind may, perhaps, be discovered by his promptitude or backwardness to comply with what is termed the fashion of dress.

> Give me, ye gods, the husband cries, an heir ;
> The teeming wife demands a daughter fair :
> The gods, too kind, nor that deny, nor this ;
> Forth comes an heir, half master and half miss.

He who can be content to follow fashion, with all her mutability, through all her revolutions, must have imbibed some of that fickleness which such a pursuit inspires. The same uncertainty which makes him fluctuate between Mr. Rag the tailor, and Mr. Blossom the habit-maker, will mark his conduct in the more serious concerns of life.

He, on the contrary, who is ridiculously precise in dress, nothing varying according to the fashion of the times, will be generally found overbearingly dogmatical in opinion. The same bigotry which condemns him to one pair of buckles, will chain him down likewise to one set of opinions. He would contend for the propriety of his dialect, though he were educated within a mile of the lake of Windermere; he would defend his taste, though he brought it from the isle of Sky; and he would dogmatize in religion, though he had his unstable principles from Birmingham.

It is a common custom from the dress and appearance of a man to guess at his trade or profession. The decency of the round curl, the gravity of the black coat, and the emblematic orthodoxy of everlasting waistcoat and breeches, are sufficient to mark a man for a defender of the faith. The laying out of the ' gravel-walk and grass-plat' in a citizen's green and gold waistcoat, will evince to an accurate observer the street in which he lives, and whether his warehouse contains the goods of an eminent shoemaker, the right pigtail of a tobacconist, or the ventures of a Turkey merchant. When we see those unaccountable combinations of ill-mixing colours, which are sometimes displayed in the coat, waistcoat, and breeches, we cannot help suspecting, that the wearer of them is by profession a fiddler not much in repute, or by trade a tailor, with no other use for his patterns than to make ' a motley suit' for himself.

It requires no great penetration to discover, that the short man, with the anchor on his button, who contends for the liberty of the press, is the midshipman of a man of war; or that the fat laughter-loving dame, all pink ribands and smiles, makes sausages in Fetter-lane, or dispenses cakes and ale at the bar of the Cross Marrow-bones, near Mile-end turnpike.

What, after all, it may be asked, is the standard of propriety in dress?—There is, perhaps, none. His own judgment and understanding must be the guide of every one. And it may not be useless to remember, that from the outward appearance people form opinions of the inward man; that he will excite indignation, whose whole mind is visibly laid out upon his dress, as certainly as the professed drunkard will disgust, whose face is like the south aspect of a garden-wall, hung with ripe fruit. He who, perhaps, owes the poverty of his understanding to his own neglect, will in vain endeavour to repair his consequence and dignity by the assistance of the graces and the tailors; all they can do for him is, to render his folly more apparent, and himself more ridiculous.

Moderation is, perhaps, no where a more positive virtue than in dress, to which no man of sense will devote the whole of his time, and no reasonable man will refuse some portion of it.—Monro.

Nº 15. SATURDAY, JUNE 23, 1787.

————Nimis alta sapit,
Bellua multorum capitum.

In a society, instituted for the purpose of amicable disputation, to which I once found means to obtain admittance, the following question was proposed for discussion :—'Which circumstances would be more irksome to a gentleman of delicate feelings; the reflection that he had killed another in a duel, or had

been himself pulled by the nose from Penzance in
Cornwall to our town of Berwick-upon-Tweed, by
way of London.' That his audience might have as
clear a comprehension as possible of the subject to
be discussed, the leader of the debate thought it necessary to specify to them the distance between the
two places mentioned, in which his accuracy was
questioned by a gentleman with his handkerchief
under his wig. The contest was carried on with
violence and acrimony, but was at length somewhat
appeased by means of a third person, who, upon
bringing the parties to explain, discovered that they
had made their calculations upon different principles,
the one having consulted Paterson's book of roads,
the other, Ogilby's.

It was on all sides sagaciously concluded upon
that one must be wrong: but it was impossible to
ascertain which, without examining the comparative excellencies of Messrs. Paterson and Ogilby,
each of whom was extolled by either party as a literary Colossus. This gave the debate another interesting turn; and as I found the heat of the room
and the contest likely to endanger my welfare, and
produce something more than a war of words, I
made as precipitate a retreat as the nature of the
case would admit; but before I could gain the door,
I found the amicable disputants had laid aside their
rhetoric and their coats, and exchanged the fanciful
and ideal shafts of wit for the material weapons of
pewter pots and oaken sticks. Never was that happy
comparison of the grammarians more thoroughly
illustrated, by which they liken logic to the clenched
fist! My escape from these logicians was a source
of comfortable contemplation, yet I could not lay
aside all my fears for the safety of those I had left
behind; however, I had the satisfaction to find the
next morning, that no material injury had been sus-

tained.   Upon turning into a shop, I bought a pair
of gloves of the Patersonian ; and soon after discovered the follower of Ogilby mending the club-
room windows.

These, and a few other circumstances, which I
need not, perhaps, enumerate, have induced me to
offer to my patient readers a few observations on
that great love of refinement and sentimentality
which is daily gaining ground among the lower orders
of our fellow-countrymen, of which nothing can I
believe radically cure them but a Dutch war.   The
grand causes of this mischief, I am inclined to suppose, are the above-mentioned pewter-pot spouting
clubs, and those rhapsodies of nonsense which are
so liberally poured upon the public, under the title
of Sentimental Novels, utterly subversive of common sense, and not very warm friends to common
honesty.   There is a fascinating power in nonsense,
which may sometimes afford relaxation, if not amusement, to a man of sense ; but which always meets
with something congenial to itself in meaner capacities.   For such capacities such compositions are
well adapted ; and for these the furrow is left unfi-
nished, and 'the hammers miss their wonted stroke.'

Some of my readers may, perhaps, be not only
readers of novels, but writers of them.   Though I
do not consider myself as qualified in any particular
to dictate to so respectable a part of the community,
yet I cannot forbear offering a few, perhaps errone-
ous, remarks upon them and their productions.

While the writers of novels have so many admirable models, upon which their style might be formed,
it is not without regret that we turn over the insipid
pages which are thrust into our sight in every book-
seller's shop.   They seem to have forgotten that
there are writers better than themselves ; that if we
wish for delicate and refined sentiment, we can recur

to Grandison and Clarissa; if we would see the
world more perhaps as it is, than as it should be, we
have Joseph Andrews and Tom Jones; or that we
can find the happy mixture of satire and moral tendency in the Spiritual Quixote and Cecilia.

I cannot help noticing the glaring impropriety they
are guilty of, who make their nobility and their pea-
sants speak the same language. They defend themselves, no doubt, by the authority and example of
Virgil's Shepherds, Sanazarius's Fishermen, and the
rustics of Mr. Pope. But when they are told, that
to copy the deformities of good writers will be no
embellishment to bad ones, they may perhaps cease
to overwhelm us with the sentimentality of their Abi-
gails, the heroic gallantry of their footmen, and the
rhetorical flourishes of their shoemakers. These are
more particularly the characters which do a material
injury to that part of the nation, who, when they have
shut up shop, wet their thumbs and spell through a
novel. A love-sick chambermaid is enough to ruin
half the sisterhood; an intriguing apprentice is the
torment of master tradesmen; and the high-flown
notions of honour, which are inculcated by " Johnny
with his shoulder-knot," will set a couple of tailors a
duelling. If the rapid course of these grievances be
not checked, we shall have the epicure justly complaining that he can get no lamb to eat with his as-
paragus, from the sensibility of the Leadenhall-
butchers; or that the melting tenderness of the cooks
prevents the eels from being skinned, or the lobsters
boiled alive. Should delicacy of thinking become
too common, we may drive the lawyers from their
quibbles, and how then are we to get those little odd
jobs done for ourselves and our estates, so convenient for our families, and so beneficial to our landed
interests? Suppose, moreover, the Jews (I do not
mean particularly those to whom Dr. Priestley's invi-

tation is directed), but the money-lenders and the proprietors of the crucible, should be infected with this growing sense of honour; the gaming-table must be deserted; there would be no market for stolen watches; and the triumph of sentiment would be the downfal of the nation.

There is much perhaps to be complained of in other publications which tend to disseminate the glare and tinsel of false sentiment; I mean the works of those imitators of Sterne, whose pages are polluted with ribaldry and dashes; and those compilers of modern tragedies, at which no man weeps, unless in pure friendship for the author.

If I in the playhouse saw a huge blacksmith-like looking fellow blubbering over the precious foolery of Nina, I should immediately take it for granted he came in with an order, and look upon his iron tears as a *forgery*. Indeed, might I be allowed to dictate upon such an occasion, no man should be permitted to moisten a white handkerchief at the *ohs* and the *ahs* of a modern tragedy, unless he possessed an estate of seven hundred a year, clear of mortgage, and every other encumbrance. Such people have a right to fling away their time as they please; the works of the loom receive no impediment from their idleness, and it is at least an innocent though insipid amusement.

While I seem endeavouring to harden the hearts of my country against those attacks which are made upon them from the stage, I am far from wishing to rob them of that prompt benevolence which is a leading feature in our national character. But I am afraid of refinement even in our virtues. I am afraid lest the same eye which is so prone to give its tributary tear to the well-told history of fancied woe, should be able to look upon real misery without emotion, because its tale is told without plot, incident, or or-

nament. I would only therefore remind those fair
ladies and well-dressed gentlemen who frequent our
theatres because they have nothing else to do, or that
they may enjoy the luxury of shedding tears with
Mrs. Siddons, that if they will look round among
their fellow-creatures, they will find their time rather
too short, than too long, for the exercise of their compassion in alleviating the distresses of their neighbours : and they may, by these means, be supplied
with luxuries, which will never reproach them with
time squandered away, or mispent in idleness or
vice,   MONRO.

N° 16.   SATURDAY, JUNE 30, 1787.

Gaudetque viam fecisse ruinâ.—LUCAN.

WITH a view, no doubt, of more deeply interesting
our attention, it seems the practice of modern tragedy
writers to aim at exciting terror by a general, yet indiscriminate recourse to the bowl and the dagger ;
whilst, after exhausting the whole armory of the property room, the fifth act is frequently accelerated from
the mere want of surviving personages to support the
play. The modern hero of the drama, seems, as it
were, professionally to consider killing as no murder ;
the rout of armies, the capture of thousands, and the
downfal of empires, forms the nauseous yet perpetual chit-chat of the narrative. However gross may
be the deficiencies of plot, character, style, and language, incident pregnant with devastation and blood-
shed is deemed a receipt in full for every excellence ;
and in proportion as the ordinary standard of human
actions is exceeded, the nearer, in the opinion of the

author, the piece approaches to perfection. Such a conduct, however, betrays the greatest poverty of expedient, and not unfrequently defeats its own end, by exciting disgust instead of approbation. Nature deals in no such hyperboles; to the credit of herself and the comfort of her creation, she as rarely shews in the moral world, a Nero, a Borgia, a Cromwell, or a Catiline, as she does in the natural, a comet or a hurricane, an earthquake or an inundation. Whoever has cursorily turned over the dramatic works of Lee and Dryden, will acknowledge the justness of this charge.

With uniform and unexampled characters, either of vice or virtue in the extreme, the aggregate of mankind are little affected; as they cannot come under their observation in real life, they have few claims to their notice, and none to their belief, in fictitious representations. Mixed characters alone come home to the minds of the multitude. The angelic qualities of a Grandison or a Harlowe are reflected but by the hearts of a few solitary individuals; whilst those of Jones find a never-failing mirror in the greater part of mankind: at all events, if it is impossible to avoid verging to one extreme or the other, the side of virtue, it is hoped, is the most probable, and, therefore, the most proper of the two; and wherever we are tempted by a story, peculiarly adapted to the tragic Muse (carrying with it, at the same time, a sufficiency of the terrible), it is the business of the poet to be most cautious in the selection, and to deal out death and destruction as reluctantly and as seldom as the nature of the incidents will admit; for I cannot help concurring with Jonathan Wild in opinion, that mischief is much too precious a commodity to be squandered.

The judiciously blending the lights and shades of a character, so as to make the one necessarily result

from, and fall into, the other, constitutes one of the
most difficult branches of the art; and in the works
of common writers, it is in vain we look for an effect
of the kind.   To delineate, with exactness, the temporary lapse of the good from virtue to vice, or those
peculiar situations in which the wicked man falters
in his career, and blushes to find himself "stagger-
ing upon virtue," demands the hand of a master.   A
character of uninterrupted detestation can scarcely
exist; and when it is obtruded upon us, we have a
right to question the abilities of him who drew it.
The Satan of Milton, though with a heart distended
with pride, and rejoicing in disobedience, when mar-
shalling his troops (all of whom had forfeited heaven in his cause), for the express purpose of confront-
ing the Almighty, betrays emotions almost incom-
patible with his nature.   They are singularly affecting :—

> ————cruel his eye, but cast
> Signs of remorse and passion, to behold
> The fellows of his crime, the followers rather,
> (Far other once beheld in bliss) condemn'd
> For ever now to have their lot in pain;
> Millions of spirits for his fault amerc'd
> Of heaven, and from eternal splendours flung
> For his revolt——

Mark the effect :

> ———— he now prepared
> To speak ————
> Thrice he assay'd, and thrice, in spite of scorn,
> Tears, such as angels weep, burst forth——
>
> BOOK i. 604, &c.

Nor has Virgil suffered the unnatural and aban-
doned Mezentius, equally the contemner of the
gods, and the enemy of man, to leave us without
exciting some pity, however undeserved.   The grief
with which he hears the death of his amiable son
Lausus announced, and the eagerness with which

he instantly hastens to revenge it; the magnanimity he discovers in his last words, in reply to the taunts of Æneas; afford a fine relief to that horror and detestation which the former part of his character had previously excited: the whole is a masterpiece in its kind.*

In the Medea of Euripides, one of the first performances antiquity has left us, it is the aim of the poet, throughout, to make Medea an object of commiseration; and to this end, he has made a tender and unremitted solicitude for the fate of her children the leading feature of her character; and on comparing the provocation on the one side with the revenge on the other, we shall find them by no means disproportioned. High-born, impatient, and ardent in her attachment, with a sensibility tremblingly alive to feel her wrongs, and a spirit to the utmost to revenge them, she is still a tender mother, though no longer a fond wife, and in every respect perfectly human. For Jason, she had forsaken and betrayed her father and her country; killed her brother Absyrtus—through his means she had been insulted by Creon, and banished his kingdom; Creon, the very man whose daughter Creusa had usurped her bed, and alienated the affections of her husband. Yet every writer who has employed himself on this subject since the Greek bard, seems widely to have mistaken, or wilfully to have departed, from what should have been their model. Seneca, with some few slight exceptions, has divested her of every claim to pity; Corneille has done the same; and Glover, a poet of our own, has left the blunder as he found it. Whoever is desirous of being made acquainted with some of the most poignant struggles between the desire of revenge and

* See from line 833 to the conclusion of the 10th Æneid.

maternal affection, is more particularly referred to this play*.

It may not be amiss to conclude these remarks with a few extracts from a most excellent modern performance, where the author has committed an error (of which he was probably sensible at the time), in order to avoid exceeding, what he seems to have considered the regular boundaries of human depravity.

In the last scene of the *Revenge*, where the dreadful unravelment of the plot takes place, through the immediate agency of Zanga himself, the following circumstances are thus forcibly unfolded:

> Thy wife is guiltless; that's one transport to me;
> And *I*, *I* let thee know it, that's another:
> *I* urged Don Carlos to resign his mistress;
> *I* forged the letter; *I* disposed the picture;
> *I* hated, *I* despised, and *I* destroy.

By these aggravations of malevolence, the detestation of the audience is worked up to the highest possible pitch: in the subsequent part of the scene, Alonzo is racked with a still farther discovery of the reasons that incited Zanga to revenge, from Zanga himself; in an agony of despair, he stabs himself, and dies; and the poet concludes the piece with endeavouring to draw a shade over the character of the Moor, before he leaves him to the mercy of the spectator; and, by one speech, aims at an atonement for him, in opposition to the detestation and disgust he had previously so successfully excited. Zanga approaches the body, and thus speaks:

> Is this Alonzo? where's his haughty mien?
> Is that the hand which smote me? Heavens! how pale!
> And art thou dead? So is my enmity;
> I war not with the dust: the great, the proud,

* See Medea, 1021, 1069, 1244, &c. &c.

> The conqueror of Africa, was my foe.
> A lion preys not upon carcases.
> This was the only method to subdue me.
> Terror and doubt fall on me ; all thy good
> Now blazes ; all thy guilt is in the grave.
> Never had man such funeral applause ;
> If I lament thee, sure thy worth was great.
> O Vengeance ! I have followed thee too far ;
> And, to receive me, Hell blows all her fires.

Zanga might here, with propriety, retort upon Young the very words which were put into his mouth in addressing Alonzo : ‘ Christian, thou mistakest my character.’

For these symptoms of repentance and regret which he here discovers, in acknowledging his having gone too great lengths in his pursuit of revenge, and that he had followed vengeance too far, are totally out of place, and unnatural ; they are against the tenets of that religion which he is supposed to profess, and the practice and example of his country, which consider a contrary conduct as eminently meritorious. The plain rule of Horace should certainly, to have completed the piece, have been here strictly adhered to :

> ——Servetur ad imum
> Qualis ab incepto processerit, aut sibi constet.—

C.   HEADLEY.

Nº 17. SATURDAY, JULY 7, 1787.

Est natura hominum novitatis avida.

THAT with respect of news, as well as of liquors, Man is a thirsty soul, we are taught in the words of my motto, at the very first entrance on our ele-

mentary studies. Curiosity is the appetite of the
mind : it must be satisfied, or we perish.

Among the improvements, therefore, of modern
times, there is none on which I find more reason to
congratulate my countrymen, than the increase of
knowledge by the multiplication of newspapers.

With what a mixture of horror and commiseration
do we now look back to that period in our history,
when, as it is said, a written letter came down once
a-week to the coffee-house, where a proper person,
with a clear and strong voice, was pitched upon to
read it aloud to the company assembled upon the
occasion ! How earnestly did they listen ! How
greedily did they suck down every drop of intelligence that fell within their reach ! Happy the man
who carried off but half a sentence ! It was his
employment, for the rest of the evening, to imagine
what the other half might have been. In days like
these, there was, indeed (if we may use the expression), ' a famine in the land;' and one wonders
how people contrived to keep body and soul together.

The provision at present made for us is ample.
There are morning papers for breakfast; there are
evening papers for supper ;—I beg pardon—I mean
dinner ; and, lest, during the interval, wind should
get into the stomach, there is, I believe, I know
there *was*—a paper published by way of luncheon,
about noon. That fanaticism may not overwhelm
us, and that profane learning may be duly mingled
with sacred, there is, also, a Sunday gazette; which
removes one objection formerly urged, and, surely,
not without reason, against the observation of the
day.

Some have complained, that to read all the newspapers, and compare them accurately together, as
it is necessary to do, before a right judgment can

be formed of the state of things in general, is grown
to be a very laborious task, which whoever per-
forms properly, can do nothing else. And why
should he? Perhaps, he has nothing else to do;
perhaps, if he had, he would not do it; or, perhaps, if he had not this to do, he would be in mischief: the complaint springs from a very criminal
indolence, the child of peace and wealth. No man
knows what may be done within the compass of a
day till he tries: fortune favours the brave: let him
buckle to the work, and despair of nothing: the
more difficulty, the more honour. The Athenians,
we are told, spent their time only ' in hearing or
telling some new thing.' Would he wish to spend
his time better than the Athenians did?

It has been thought, that tradesmen and artifi-
cers may spend too much of their time in this employment, to the neglect of their own respective
occupations : but this can be thought only by such
as have not considered, that to an Englishman, his
country is every thing. Self is swallowed up, as it
ought to be, in patriotism : or, to borrow ecclesi-
astical language, the constitution is his diocess ;
his own business can only be regarded in the light
of a *commendam*, on which, if he cast an eye now
and then, as he happens to pass that way, it is
abundantly sufficient.

The spirit of defamation, by which a newspaper
is often possessed, has now found its own remedy
in the diversity of them : for though a gentleman
may read that he himself is a scoundrel, and his
wife no better than she should be to-day, he will
be sure to read that both of them are very good
sort of people to-morrow. In the same manner,
if one paper, through mistake or design, kill his
friend, there is another ready to fetch him to life ;
nay, if he have good luck in the order of his read-

ing, he may be informed that his friend is alive
again before he had perused the account of his
death.

The expense of advertising in so many different
newspapers, may, perhaps, be deemed a hardship
upon authors: but then they have, in return, the
comfort of reflecting, what benefactors they are to
the revenue: besides, how easy is it for them to
balance the account, by printing with a large type,
due space between the lines, and a broad margin!
Great advantage may be obtained by throwing their
compositions into the form of letters, which may be
as short as they please; and a reader of delicacy
thinks, the shorter the better. A letter of six lines
is a very decent letter: it may begin at the bottom
of one page, and end at the top of the next; so that
eight parts in ten of what the reader purchases,
consist of blank paper: his eye is agreeably relieved; and if the paper be good for any thing, he
has, upon the whole, no bad bargain.

That the vehicles of intelligence, numerous as
they are, yet are not too numerous, appears, because there is news for them all, there are pur-
chasers for all, and advertisements for all: these
last not only afford aid to government, and are
pretty reading, but sometimes have an influence
upon the important affairs of the world, which is
not known, or even suspected.

No event, of latter times, has more astonished
mankind, than the sudden downfal of the Jesuits:
and various causes have been assigned for it. I am
happy that it is in my power, by means of a correspondent at Rome, who was in the secret, to furnish
my readers with a true one:—an anecdote, which,
I believe, has never before transpired.

It was owing, then, to an advertisement in an
English newspaper, which passed over to the conti-

nent, and, by some means or other, found its way
to the Vatican. I remember, perfectly well, to
have read the advertisement at the time, and to
have noted it down in my adversaria, as I am wont
to do when any thing strikes me in a particular
manner. It ran thus :

' John Haynes, of St. Clements, Oxford, begs
leave to inform the public, that he alone possesses
the true art of " *making leather breeches fit easy.*" '

As the newspaper containing the advertisement
came from Oxford, his Holiness and their Eminences
immediately saw, that in these last words was conveyed a keen though covert satire upon the *loose
casuistry* of the sons of Loyola. A consistory was
called, and Ganganelli formed his resolution :—what
followed, all the world knows.

I thought it but justice to my worthy friend
Haynes, to mention thus much ; and, as by the introduction of fustian, his trade has long been upon
the decline, I would hope that every good Protes-
tant will forthwith bespeak a pair of leather breeches
(and pay for them when brought home) of a man
who has given such a blow to Popery, and had the
address to effect what the Provincial Letters attempted in vain.

From this instance, it is evident, that we ought to
read all newspapers, country as well as town, on
which we can lay our hands ; for we know not what
we may have lost by missing any one of them. This
enlarges the sphere of our researches, and the imagination riots in the delicious prospect. The jour-
nals printed at the two universities must always have
an especial claim to our attention.

I was seized, a few years ago, at a considerable
distance from our Alma Mater, with a violent fever.
James's powder ceased to be of service ; the physician of the place, who had been called in, shook his

head; and I began to think I should never more behold St. Mary's spire, and Radcliffe's library. I
was almost speechless, but endeavoured, from time
to time, as well as I could, to articulate the word
Jackson. My attendants concluded me delirious,
and heeded not what I said; till a lad, who travelled
as my servant, coming accidentally into the room,
exclaimed eagerly, that he would be hanged if his
master did not mean the Oxford newspaper. It was
fetched by express, and I made signs that it should
be read. The effect was a kindly perspiration, followed by a gentle sleep, from which I awoke with
my fever abated, and felt myself greatly refreshed
indeed. I continued mending. On the Saturday
following, ' the julep, as before,' was repeated; and
on Monday I arose, and pursued my journey.

There is one argument in favour of a multiplicity
of newspapers, which I do not remember to have
met with; namely, that no man is ever satisfied with
another man's reading a newspaper to him; but the
moment it is laid down, he takes it up, and reads it
over again. It is absolutely necessary, therefore,
that each should have a newspaper to himself, and
so change round, till every paper shall have been read
by every person.

A question has sometimes been debated concerning the best time for reading newspapers: but,
surely, the proper answer to it is, ' read them the
moment you can get them.' For my own part, I always dry my paper upon my knees, and make shift
to pick out a few articles during the operation. It
has been fancied, that by reading of this kind in a
morning (the season marked out for it since Mr. Pal-
mer's regulation of the post), the head of a young
academic becomes so filled with a heterogeneous mixture of trash, that he is fit for nothing: but—*bona
verba,*—Fair and softly, my good friend. Why should

we not take up the matter at the other end, and say, rather, his mind is so expanded by a rich variety of new ideas, that he is fit for—any thing?

I shall conclude this speculation with observing, that we have just cause to be thankful for the number of newspapers dispersed among us, since, in a little time, nothing else will be read; it being nearly agreed by all persons of the ton, that is, by all men of sense and taste, that religion is a *hum*, virtue a *twaddle*, and learning a *bore*.—Z.

BISHOP HORNE.

Nº 18.   SATURDAY, JULY 14, 1787.

Tempus edax rerum veteres cecinêre poëtæ;
  At nostrum tempus quis negat esse bibax?—ANON.

Of *Eating* time old poets rhyme,
But ours is, surely, *Drinking* time.

AGAINST drunkenness there are, perhaps, no arguments so strong as those which may be collected from the songs of Bacchanals. We are dissuaded from it by the moralist, who represents it as the fascination of a Siren, which wins us over to vice, by subduing our reason; and we are invited to it by the song of the Bacchanal, as something which will soothe our cares; inspire us with joys vehement, if not permanent; and banish from our minds the evils and the troubles of life. The former seems to think that this vice has so many allurements, as to require his cautions against our being seduced by it; and the latter, that it has so few, as to stand in need of his recommendation of it.

Fecundi calices quem non fecêre disertum?
Contractâ quem non in paupertate solutum?—HORACE.

Wine can to poverty content dispense,
Or tip the stammering tongue with eloquence.

In reasoning, these words will go no farther than
to prove, that he who is poor, may, by drinking, become in imagination rich; or that he who stammers,
may, by the same expedient, find the temporary use
of his tongue. The man who is not poor then will
recollect, that he stands in no need of such a receipt;
and he who does not stammer, will think that remedy unnecessary which was intended to cure a disease by which he is not afflicted. I can, moreover,
inform them, upon pretty good authority, that this
medicine has made many a rich man poor, and de-
prived many an orator of his speech.

Drunkenness is farther recommended to us as the
inspirer of courage,—*In prælio trudit inermem,*—it
thrusts the unarmed man to battle.—That it has this
effect, is, I believe, very true, and so much the worse
for the unarmed man. The testimony of a black eye,
or a bloody nose, the frequent offsprings of a drunken
frolic, are striking proofs, that to go unarmed to battle is no great mark of wisdom or desirable courage.

There are many persons in the world, who measure a man's qualities by his capacity to hold wine;
the religion of these good people is a bottle of port,
their wit a thump on the back, and their jokes upon
the whole, no laughing matter. They are, however,
so honest, and so disagreeable, that a reasonable
man will do any thing to serve them, and any thing
to avoid their company. I may, perhaps, incur the
charge of being envious, when I declare, that I have
very little satisfaction in the presence of him whose
only boast is, that he is a better man than myself by
two bottles. Wine, however, inspires confidence,

wit, and eloquence ; that is, it changes modesty to impudence, ingrafts the art of joking upon dulness, and makes a story-teller of a fool. While these qualifications are worth attaining, I would have sobriety considered as a vulgarity, if not stigmatized as a vice ; but when that ceases to be the case, I hope the liberal spirit of tolerating principles, which is so much the fashion of the age, will allow a moderate man, without infamy, to say, ‘ I would rather not get very drunk to-day.’ Indeed, I have reason to believe this might be brought to pass, having seen a gentleman, with great politeness, excused from taking his wine, upon his producing a testimony from his physician, that he then laboured under a violent fever ; or a certificate from churchwardens of the parish, properly authenticated, to testify that his aunt was dead.

I have often supposed, that there must be some disgrace or impropriety in habitual drunkenness, from the many excuses which are framed by persons who indulge themselves in it. I know a fond couple (fond, I mean, of liquor) who are continually, ‘ from eve to morn, from morn to dewy eve,’ deluging their thirsty souls in gin and water.—Mr. Morgan excuses himself, because he has lost money in the alley ; and poor Mrs. Morgan complains of a perpetual coldness at her stomach. Some people find an excuse for drinking in the loss of their wives, in which they are happily aided by the proverb, that ‘ sorrow is dry.’ Others drink to dissipate the cares and solicitudes of matrimony ; and others, because they cannot be admitted to a portion of such cares and solicitudes. Sufficient argument, therefore, may be found, to make a notable and legitimate drunkard of the bachelor, the married man, or the widower. It is difficult to ascertain amongst what class of people this accomplishment is in the highest repute. A first minister must have hours of relaxation, and a first minister's footman those of entertainment : to accomplish which, the former has a right, if he pleases, to get ' drunk as a piper;' and the latter, by the same rule, ' drunk as a lord.'

From the proverbial phrase, which I have had occasion to quote, ' drunk as a piper,' and other circumstances, I am led to conjecture, that the science of drinking has been cultivated with particular success among musicians,

> Queis *liquidam* pater
> Vocem cum citharâ dedit.

To whom Apollo has given,

> To whet their whistle, and handle the lyre.

The great man, whose musical talents are annually noised in Westminster-abbey, was no less the votary of Bacchus than of Apollo ; and from a late newspaper we learn, that Mr. Abel, the celebrated performer, amidst the joys of wine, either being little skilled in our language, or having drunk until he was unable to speak any, caught up his *viol de Gamba*, and with great execution and good humour obliged the company with the story of Le Fevre. Such a story so told to a man of quick apprehension, a good ear, and tolerably drunk, must, no doubt, have proved a recreation interesting and entertaining. Yet I cannot but rejoice, that there are many people in the world who still continue to use the old way of telling stories by word of mouth, and who can join in a conversation without thinking it necessary to have recourse to F *sharp*.

I am, however, no judge of these matters, and think it right to confess that I am no musician ; and that the enthusiastic raptures of a drunken fiddler convey to my mind no ideas of the true sublime.

Those great geniuses who are not thoroughly satisfied with being vicious, unless they can find precedents for their vice, may drink on under the sanction and authority of Alcæus, Aristophanes, and Ennius. Dulness may still plead a right to this indulgence, because the unsteady principles of heathen morality did not stigmatise it in Cato. I have already produced examples, under which all musicians, poets, satirists, and great wits, may shelter themselves; and I will undertake to furnish the same kind of license for the barbers, the dentists, the carpenters, the glaziers, or any other order of men who will depute an embassy to call upon me: —I shall only request, in return, that they will allow me a trifling consideration in their respective branches. I shall stipulate for a triple bob-major, because Demosthenes shaved his head; and to have my teeth drawn, because that orator had an impediment in his speech; I must have a wooden leg, because Agesilaus was lame; and a pair of glass eyes, because Homer was blind. I shall at least be supplied with as rational apologies for my deformity, as they will for their drunkenness; and, in process of time, I have no doubt, but it will be considered as highly ornamental to be bald-pated, fluttering, limping, and blear-eyed.

To say nothing of the immorality of drunkenness, I cannot look upon it as the accomplishment of a gentleman. It seems to me to be in the same class of polite sciences with quoits, cock-fighting, tobacco-chewing, and quarter-staff.

If we examine the character of Falstaff, in whom all the bewitching qualities of a professed drunkard are exhibited, we shall find it such a one as few would willingly think like themselves. He has not only wit himself, but is the cause of it in other men. He manifests much good humour in bearing the raillery of others, and great quickness in retorts of his own. He drinks much; and, while he enumerates the qualities of your true sherris, he skilfully commends what he drinks. Yet the same character is as strongly represented to us, a parasite, an unseasonable joker, a liar, a coward, and a dishonest man.

There are, perhaps, some few circumstances under which the liberal use of wine may be more easily excused; but, while we furnish palliatives for vice, we only multiply the means to cheat ourselves.

I shall conclude this paper with a few remarks on the character of the drunkard, from a pleasant writer* of the last century :—

' A drunkard (says he) is in opinion a good fellow, in practise a living conduit; his vices are like errata in the latter end of a false coppie, they point the way to vertue by setting downe the contrary. There is some affinity betwixt him and a chamelion; he feeds upon ayre, for he doth eate his word familiarly. He cannot run fast enough to prove a good footman; for ale and beere (the heaviest element next earth) will overtake him. His nose, the most innocent, beares the corruption of his other senses folly; from it may bee gathered the emblem of one falsely scandal'd, for *it* not offending is colourably punish'd. A beggar and hee are both of one stocke, but the beggar claims antiquity. The beggar begs that he may drink, and hath his meaning; the other drinks that he may beg, and shall have the true meaning shortly,' &c.   MONRO.

---

* John Stephens the younger, of Lincoln's-inn, 1615.

Nᵒ 19. SATURDAY, JULY 21, 1787.

Rudis indigestaque moles.

MANY of my readers will, perhaps, compare this day's provision to the Saturday's dinner of a notable housewife, composed of beef-steaks, and the fragments of the week. I wish them rather to consider it as an entertainment, to the furnishing of which the presents of my friends have principally contributed, and wherein it only remains for me to place the dishes on the table.

'TO THE AUTHOR OF THE OLLA PODRIDA.

'DEAR SIR,

'I be a baker's daughter, and, to tell you the truth, so much in love you can't think. Now, Sir, as you seems to be a grave sort of a gentleman, I dares to say you can read the hand, cast nativities, tell fortunes, and all that. What now do you think, Sir, I will give you, if so be that you will tell me for certain whether or no I shall have Dick? why fourteen kisses, and that's a baker's dozen you know; and so no more from yours, till I'm married,

PATTY PENNYLESS.'

To this fair lady the author of the Olla Podrida has only to reply, that he is not a conjurer, nor indeed does he wear a wig. However, by consulting his books, he has discovered a few negative maxims, by the observance of which his correspondent may *have Dick* if Dick be worth her having.—Should he be extravagant in the praise of her beauty, she is advised not to believe him; should he offer her a green

gown, not to accept it. In the disposal of her
baker's dozens, not to be profuse; and, moreover,
not to be any person's till she is married, not even
her well-wisher's, and so no more.—TARATALLA.

'TO THE AUTHOR OF THE OLLA PODRIDA.

'GOOD SIR,

'I am an old soldier, and, though I say it, have seen
and felt as much hard service as any man, and have
actually fought as long as I had limbs to support
me. My legs, Sir, which at this present writing are
no less than fourteen hundred English miles asunder,
are buried (for aught I know) in two different quarters of the globe, and will, alas! never cross each
other again. I have a hand, Sir, in two great kingdoms, whose names, for politic reasons, I think proper at present to conceal, and only add, that it is
no impossible thing for a man to be in one country,
and at the same time to have a hand in another.
Such is my situation, Sir, that I am cropped close
like a Buckinghamshire pollard, and have hardly a
twig left upon my trunk. Now, Sir, there is a knot
of merry gentlemen in our neighbourhood, who,
forsooth, having legs and arms of their own natural
growth, are pleased to be considerably witty on
what is left of me, and not unfrequently extend
their pleasantry to the ascititious branches which
are engrafted upon me. I request, through the medium of your paper, Sir, that you will inform these
wags, that my arms and legs are formed from the
same piece, and not of different kinds of timber, as
they have maliciously reported; and that although
I wear my common crab-trees on common occasions,
I have a pair of best mahogany supporters for red-
letter days and Sundays. I am the more desirous
of their being informed of these particulars, as I

pay my addresses to a well-favoured middle-aged
lady of some fortune in the village; and I would
have you, her, them, and all the world, to know,
that I never was so ill bred as to pay her any compliment on my common legs, nor did I ever venture
upon a salute but upon mahogany. I am informed
by my man who takes me to pieces, and puts me together again every night and morning, that these
merry men stick at nothing to ridicule me. If you
would take my part against the sad dogs, you would
very much oblige an old general, who hath, you
find, long since laid down his arms, and is no longer
able to lift up a hand against any coward who pre-
sumes upon his incapability to affront him.

JOHN CROP.'

I hope I have taken the most effectual method to
remedy Mr. Crop's grievances, by stating his account of them.

MONRO.—CROP's Letter by LEYCESTER.

'TO THE AUTHOR OF THE OLLA PODRIDA.

'SIR,

'It has pleased Providence to build this vessel of
mine of such crazy materials, that a blast or two
of wind from the east-north-east quite oversets me.
No sooner does the weathercock which is erected
on the cupola of my pigeon-house point at east,
but the rheumatic pains, pins and needles, cramps,
joint aches, pinches, contractions, twinges, and the
sciatica, attack me in all my quarters. Whether
our bodies, which, I cannot help sometimes thinking, are made for many ends, designs, and purposes,
whereof we are at present ignorant, may not serve
as inns and baiting-places for swarms of insects
which are at such times on their journey to unknown

regions, or whether these piercing blasts bring down
upon us wretched mortals numberless invisible
spears, arrows, knives, and swords, which acted upon
by the force of the wind, sheath themselves deep
in our muscles, bones, and joints, I must leave, Sir, to
you and the learned world to determine. These ills
very frequently put my thoughts, as well as limbs,
to the rack, to discover their real springs and causes,
and I often meditate upon this matter, until conceits
of no very common shape and form are most equi-
vocally generated in my pericranium. Sometimes I
fancy that these guests bring with them on their
wings a very peculiar species of animalcula, which,
lighting on this our fleshy habitation, creep in like
bats and jack-daws into old castle walls through
unnumbered and imperceptible chinks, fissures, and
crannies of our rimose and rimpled carcases, where,
when they have got in, they keep a great stir-about
in quarrelling, fighting, and making love; in building nests, and depositing eggs, the productions of
which, after we have been some time buried in the
earth, leave us without an ounce of flesh to cover
us. These are strange chimeras, Sir, and make me
tremble from head to foot in my great chair. But,
Sir, while I know my house is to be swallowed down
by an earthquake, the certainty of my being out of
it, with all my treasures and valuables safe and
sound, when this accident happens, gives me an unspeakable pleasure, and a comfort at my very heart.
            I am, Sir, your humble servant,
                    JEREMY CRAZYBONES.'

The whimsical philosophy of Mr. Crazybones
seems to me to border on that pleasant melancholy
humour which sober rationality sometimes denomi-
nates madness. When it is properly ascertained
that he is harmless, and in good bodily health, I

shall endeavour to prescribe a medicine for him which may serve to dissipate those chimeras which make him tremble so in his arm-chair.

' To the Author of the Olla Podrida.

' DEAR SIR,

' The Spectator and others have always thought proper to furnish the public with some description of their persons and domestic qualities. I wish you likewise would communicate to your readers, whether you are a tall or a short man; a horseback-breaker, or a pantaloon; whether you wear a wig, or your own hair, and talk much or little; with such other interesting particulars, descriptive of your character and appearance. I suppose you are neither a sloven nor a coxcomb.—Pray, Sir, are you a bachelor or a married man?　　　　Yours, &c.

　　　　　　　　　　　　　　MINUTIUS.'

For information in all these interesting particulars, I shall refer Minutius to a view of myself. If he has any skill in physiognomy, he will discover every thing he wishes, when I inform him, he may see me any morning, between five and six, going towards Joe Pullen's tree. He will know me by my red waistcoat, and a pipe in my mouth.

' To the Author of the Olla Podrida.

' SIR,

' I have a strong desire to see my writings in print, though at present I have nothing to say.— I wish, however, you would insert this in some corner of your paper, and you will much oblige

　　　　　　　　　　　　　　RICHARD BRIEF.'

MONRO.—CRAZYBONES' Letter by LEYCESTER.

Nº 20. SATURDAY, JULY 28, 1787.

'TO THE AUTHOR OF THE OLLA PODRIDA.

Falsus honos juvat.

'SIR,

' So prevailing is the love of superiority in the human breast, that the most strange and ridiculous claims are set up for it, by those who have no real merit to offer. It is, indeed, absurd enough to value oneself for bodily perfections, or mental powers, both being totally the gift of the Supreme Being, without the least merit on our part. Nor is that consequence, arrogated from illustrious birth, at all justifiable, since the proof of possessing it cannot arise higher than probability : all ladies are not Susannahs, nor all servants Josephs. But suppose it allowed ; a good man does not want that addition ; and to a bad one, the virtues of his ancestors are a standing reproach. A lower kind of importance is frequently assumed from the excellence of one's domestic animals, such as a fine pack of hounds, staunch pointers, or fleet horses, when the arrogator of their merit has neither bred, chosen, nor taught them ; and has had no other concern with them, than simply paying the purchase-money. How excellently does Dr. Young, in his Universal Passion, draw and expose a character of this kind !

> The 'squire is proud to see his courser strain,
> Or well breathed beagles sweep along the plain.
> Say, dear Hippolytus, (whose drink is ale,
> Whose erudition is a Christmas tale,
> Whose mistress is saluted with a smack,
> And friend received with thumps upon the back,)
> When thy sleek gelding nimbly leaps the mound,
> And Ringwood opens on the tainted ground,

Is that thy praise? let Ringwood's fame alone;
Just Ringwood leaves each animal his own,
Nor envies when a gipsy you commit,
And shake the clumsy bench with country wit;
When you the dullest of dull things have said,
And then ask pardon for the jest you made.

'But of all the ridiculous pretensions to pre-eminence, that arising from the place of one's residence
seems the most foolish; and nothing is more common,
and that not limited to countries, provinces, or cities,
but is regularly extended to the different parts of
this town of London, and even to the several stories
of a house. The appellation of country-booby is
very ready in the mouth of every citizen and apprentice, who feels an imaginary superiority from living
in the metropolis; and any one who has seen London ladies of the middling order, in a country church,
must have observed, that there they fail not to display a contemptuous consequence founded on their
coming from that town.

'London is divided into the suburbs, city, and
court, or, as it is styled, east of Temple-bar, and
t'other end of the town; and again subdivided into
many degrees and districts, each in a regular climax
conferring ideal dignity and precedency. The inhabitants of Kent-street and St. Giles's are mentioned
by those of Wapping, Whitechapel, Mile-end, and
the Borough of Southwark, with sovereign contempt;
whilst a Wappineer, a Mile-ender, and a Borough-
nian, are terms proverbially used, about the Exchange and Fenchurch-street, to express an inferior
order of beings; nor do the rich citizens of Lom-
bard-street ever lose the opportunity of retailing the
joke of a Whitechapel fortune. The same contempt
is expressed for the cits inhabiting the environs of
the Royal Exchange, or residing within the sound of
Bow-bell, St. Bennet's Sheerhog, Pudding-lane, and

Blow-bladder-street, by the inferior retainers of the law in Chancery-lane, Hatton-garden, and Bedford-row; and these again are considered as people living totally out of the polite circle by the dwellers in Soho, and the aspiring tradesmen settled in Bloomsbury, Queen's, and Red-Lion-squares, in the first flight from their counting-houses in Thames-street, Billingsgate, and Mark-lane. The new colonies about Oxford-street sneer at these would-be people of fashion, and are in their turns despised by those whose happier stars have placed them in Pall-Mall, St. James's, Cavendish, and Portman-squares. Thus it is, taking this criterion of pre-eminence in a general view: but to descend to a smaller scale, the lodger in the first floor scarcely deigns to return the bow of the occupier of the second in the same house, who, on all occasions, makes himself amends by speaking with the utmost contempt of the garreteers over head, with many shrewd jokes on *sky parlours*. The precedency between the garret and the cellar seems evidently in favour of the former, garrets having time out of mind been the residence of the literati, and sacred to the Muses: it is not, therefore, wonderful that the inhabitants of those sublime regions should think the renters of cellars, independent of a pun, much below them.

'Besides the distinctions of altitude, there is that of *forward* and *backward*. I have heard a lady, who lodged in the fore room of the second story, on being asked after another who lodged in the same house, scornfully describe her by the appellation of "the woman living in the back room."

'Polite situations not only confer dignity on the parties actually residing on them, but also, by emanations of gentility, in some measure ennoble the vicinity; thus persons living in any of the back lanes or courts near one of the polite squares or streets, may tack them to their address, and thereby somewhat add to their consequence. I once knew this method practised with great success by a person who lodged in a court in Holborn, who constantly added to his direction, "opposite the Duke of Bedford's, Bloomsbury-square."

'To prevent disputes respecting the superiority here treated of, I have, with much impartiality, trouble, and severe study, laid down a sort of table of precedency, and marshalled the usual places of residence in their successive order, beginning with the lowest. First, then, of those who occupy only a part of a tenement, stand, the holders of stalls, sheds, and cellars, to them succeed the residents in garrets, whence we gradually descend to the second and first floor, the dignity of each story being in the inverse ratio of its altitude; it being always remembered, that those dwelling in the fore part of the house take place of the inhabitants of the same elevation renting the back rooms; the ground floor, if not a shop or a warehouse, ranks with the second story. Situations of houses I have arranged in the following order: passages, alleys, courts, streets, rows, places, and squares. My reason for these arrangements, I may, perhaps, give on a future opportunity.

'As a comfort to those who might despond at seeing their lot placed in a humiliating degree, let them consider, that all but the first situations are capable of promotion; and that an inhabitant of a yard or court may, without moving, find himself a dweller in a street. Many instances of this have very lately occurred. Does any one now hesitate to talk of Fludyer and Crown-streets, Westminster? and yet both were, not long ago, simply Axe-yard and Crown-court, from which they have been raised to their present dignity, without passing through the

intermediate rank of lanes. In the same manner
Hedge-lane is become Whitcombe-street; and
Cumberland-court takes the title of Milford-place;
and Cranbourn-alley has experienced a similar elevation; and any one that should chance to call it
less than Cranbourn-street, would risk something
more than abuse from the ladies of the quilting
frame, and sons of the gentle craft resident there.
Tyburn-road has been created Oxford-street; and
Leicester-fields honoured with the rank, style, and
title of Leicester-square.'   GROSE.'

N° 21.   SATURDAY, AUGUST 4, 1787.

Οστις δε διαβολιαις πειθεται ταχυ,
Ητοι πονηρος αυτος εστι τους τροπους
Η πανταπασι παιδαριου γνωμην εχει.—MENANDER.

He who willingly extends his credulity to the belief of calumnies,
is a wicked man or fool.

THAT sacred weapon, Satire, so seldom falls into
hands able to wield it with fortitude and discretion,
that if we examine the characters of those who have
arrogated to themselves the office of stigmatizing
vice, the result of our labours will oftentimes prove
disappointment and regret.

Yet, as not every disappointment is without some
useful lesson, it may not, perhaps, be quite unprofitable to offer a few cursory remarks upon some of
those writers who have passed through the world
under the denomination of Satirists.

To fix a period from which satire may be supposed
to have had its beginning, is to date the origin of

that whose existence is coeval with the nature of man. The manners of all times have furnished materials for the pen of the satirist; and writers of all nations have discovered either their integrity in the proper use of it, or their malevolence in the prostitution of it. That Homer gave sufficient proofs of his abilities to become a powerful satirist, we have heard in his Margites, and we have seen in his character of Thersites.

The different regulations of the Greek comedy have been accurately and frequently stated to us; it is therefore unnecessary to give a very minute account of what every one is, or may be, so minutely acquainted with. In consequence of the licentious satire produced into public by Cratinus and Eupolis, it was decreed that no one should name another on the stage. Under these restrictions wrote Menander and Philemon, with the chastity of whose style, and the purity of whose sentiments, we have reason to lament that we cannot be more intimately acquainted. To them succeeded Aristophanes, upon whom his biographical panegyrist has been able to heap no other commendation, than such as is due to the misapplication of abilities, which might have been serviceable to his country and creditable to himself.

Let the reader of Aristophanes divest himself of his inclination to become acquainted with the customs of the Greeks, and the niceties of their language, and he will find little in that author tending to make him a wiser or a better man. While ribaldry is considered as the perfection of wit, so long shall we look for a model in Aristophanes; while the malicious exercise of superior abilities be commendable, so long shall Aristophanes be commended. The humour of this writer is generally low, and frequently obscene; his ridicule, from being misapplied, rather disgusts his reader, than vilifies his object; and that odium, which in the wickedness of his heart he would heap upon another, falls with justice upon himself. When we consider the reputed elegance even to a proverb of the Athenians, it is not without astonishment that we mark the consequence of his plays; scarce less than infatuation seems to have actuated the minds of his audience. By means of his worthless ribaldry, the finger of scorn was pointed against Æschylus, Euripides, and Sophocles; and to his too efficacious calumny Socrates paid the tribute of his life. Plutarch, in his comparison between Aristophanes and Menander, observes of the former, 'that his language is tumid, full of stage trick and illiberality, which is never the case with Menander—the man of science is offended, and vulgarity delighted. He, however, obtained popularity by exercising his wit against the taxgatherers: he is remarkable,' adds he, ' for having so distributed his speeches, that there is no difference whether a father speaks or a son, a rustic or a deity, an old man or a hero. In Menander it is directly opposite.' But the violence with which Plutarch condemns the writings of Aristophanes, may, perhaps, discover that his judgment was somewhat biassed by his indignation against the author. Thus far, however, on all sides will be readily granted; that could the fate of Menander and Aristophanes have been reversed, it is probable, comedy would have found a standard of taste instead of a precedent for licentiousness, and, using such example, would have proved herself the mirror of truth instead of the vehicle of calumny. The reader who has discretion enough to look upon Aristophanes as the skilful advocate in a bad cause, may be entertained by his writings, and not prejudiced by his opinions. But we are too apt to subscribe without examination to the dicta of acknowledged abilities:—there is little trouble in this, but much danger.

Of the Roman satirists we may speak more favourably than perhaps of any set of writers who have adorned any country. The habits of their lives in general gave a sanction to the gravity of their doctrines. The conduct of Plautus was no disgrace to his writings; Lucilius gave no precepts of virtue to others, which he did not exemplify in himself; and to that best writer of the most accomplished age, Horace, who shall deny the meed of praise, which the testimony of his own times declared his due, and the universal consent of succeeding ages has ratified and confirmed? Equal to him in strength of mind, and in virtue by no means inferior, were Juvenal and Persius: yet they had not that art and judgment, the possession of which has made Horace more read and admired, and the want of which has made themselves more neglected.

The policy of the Gauls, and the terrors of the Bastile, have, no doubt, while they carried the licentiousness of a gay and lively nation, at the same time depressed the ardour of many ingenious satirists: that this has been the case, the world has little cause to lament; since the few, who have discovered themselves in that country, seem rather desirous of establishing a reputation for themselves, than zealous for the promotion of virtue. They are content to be called good writers, without ambition to be accounted virtuous men.

In order to review some of the best satirists of our own nation, we must pass over the bigotry of one age, in which Milton seems to have presided, and the profligacy of another, in which this land exchanged the horrors of civil war, and intestine discords, for the vicious luxuries of an ill-spent peace

which were ratified by the countenance, encouragement, and example of a king. The wits of this age
were consistent in their lives and writings, and immorality was the characteristic of both. They seem
to have agreed as it were with universal consent,
that ' a tale of humour was sufficient knowledge,
good-fellowship sufficient honesty,' and a restraint
from the extremes of vice sufficient virtue.

If we descend to what has been called the Augustan age of English literature, we shall find the
satirical works of that time will not bear a very near
inspection. It is a lamentable truth, that the same
pen which had been so often and so successfully employed in the cause of virtue; which had given im-
mortality to the Man of Ross, and the compliment
of truth to Addison—was unwarily led into an attempt to pluck the laurels from the brow of Bentley,
and to gratify an unmanly malevolence in the publication of the Dunciad.

The censures of Swift seem to have been marked
by habitual ill-nature; and the compliments of
Young by an habitual want of discrimination. And
it generally happens, that the censures of such satirists, and the commendations of such panegyrists,
keep an equal balance, both weighing—nothing.

Nothing has, I believe, been more frequently an
object of ill-placed ridicule than learning, which,
before it can appear ridiculous, must be misnamed
pedantry. Every Homer has his Zoilus; and every
Zoilus, like Homer's, is remembered only to be despised. Whatever effect the attacks of Aristophanes
upon the tragedians of his day might have towards
vitiating the taste of his countrymen, posterity have
seemed willing to do justice to those works, in the
admiration of which the wisest and best men of all
ages have united.

I am inclined to believe that the learning of Dr.

Bentley lost no admirers from the attacks of Pope, or the insinuations of Swift; and an instance, taken from times nearer our own, will, perhaps, place the odium of malevolent satire in a stronger light. To the truth of this every one can bear witness, who is acquainted with those attacks which have been made by Churchill and others upon Johnson. That great writer, who, as he was a man, could not but err, and as he was a wise man, could not persist in error; who was no feeble or time-serving moralist, but the firm and systematic teacher and practiser of virtue— he has shewn us, that the shafts of malevolence may be turned aside, however keenly pointed, or however deeply empoisoned. The reader of Lexiphanes is excited to laugh without approbation; and the attack of Churchill remains a melancholy instance of prostituted wit. What shall we say of those, who, offended by no public and growing vice, provoked by no private wrongs, in deliberate wantonness sport with the characters of their neighbours, whom they hold out to unjust ridicule and unmerited reproach? It is but a weak apology for the baseness of their hearts, that the produce of their pens may afford amusement to the idle, and gratification to the malevolent. But our reflections upon this subject will be too applicable to many of those publications which are the disgrace and entertainment of the times in which we live. In the commendation of such men, let all those join who have learned, from the writings of Shaftesbury, that ridicule is the test of truth; or from the conduct of Voltaire, that calumny is a cardinal virtue.　　　MONRO.

N° 22. SATURDAY, AUGUST 11, 1787.

The Briton still with fearful eye foresees
What storm or sunshine Providence decrees;
Knows for each day the weather of our fate.
A quidnunc is an almanack of state.

YOUNG'S Satires.

AMONG the various employments which engage the
attention of mankind, it is not unpleasant to consider their topics of conversation.   Every country has
some peculiar to itself, which, as they derive their
origin from the establishment of custom and the pre-
dominance of national pride, are permanent in their
duration, and extensive in their influence.   Like
standing dishes, they form the most substantial part
of the entertainment, and are served up at the tables
both of the rich and the poor.   The Dutchman talks
incessantly of the bank of Amsterdam, the Italian of
the carnival, the Spaniard of a bull-fight, and the
English of politics and the weather.

That these last-mentioned topics should gain so
great an ascendancy over the Englishman, is by no
means a subject of wonder.   In a country, where
the administration may be changed in half a year,
and the weather may alter in half a minute, the
quick and surprising vicissitudes must necessarily
rouse the attention, and furnish the most obvious
materials for conversation.   From the influence of
that gravity which is remarked by foreigners to be
the characteristic of the inhabitants of Britain, they
are disposed to view these endemial subjects in a
gloomy light, and to make them the parents of sullen
dissatisfaction and ideal distress.   John Bull, with
a contracted brow, and surly voice, complains that
we have April in July, and that the greatest patriots

are shamefully kept out of place. All this may be very true ; but, if his worship could be persuaded to confess his feelings, he would acknowledge, that the gratification of complaining is far from inconsiderable ; and that if these topics, on which he vents his spleen, were taken from him, little would remain to occupy his mind, or set his tongue in motion.

Let us indulge, for a moment, the whimsical supposition, that our climate was changed for that of Italy, and our government for that of the Turks ; the consequences are easy to be foreseen—a general silence would reign throughout the island, from Port Patrick to the Land's End ; and we should be all well qualified for the school of Pythagoras. Our silence, indeed, would scarcely be limited, like that of his scholars, to five years. Every house in England would resemble the monastery of La Trappe, where the monks are no better than walking statues. The only talkers among us would be physicians, lawyers, old maids, and travellers. The physician might fatigue us with his *materia medica*, the lawyer with his *qui tam* actions, the old maid with difficult cases at cards, and the traveller with the dimensions of the Louvre, without fear of interruption or contradiction. We should look up to them as students do to professors reading lectures, and, like poor Dido, feel a pleasure in the encouragement of loquacity.

> Illacosque iterum demens audire labores
> Exposcit, pendetque iterum narrantis ab ore.

> She fondly begs him to repeat once more
> The Trojan story that she heard before ;
> Then to destruction charm'd in rapture hung
> On every word, and died upon his tongue.—PITT.

The game at whist would be played with uninterrupted tranquillity, and the cry of silence in the courts of justice might be omitted without the small-

XLI.　　　　　　　　　M

est inconvenience. In short, all the English who
went abroad would be entitled to the compliment
which was once paid a nobleman at Paris. A lively
French marquis, after having been a whole evening
in his company without hearing him utter a syllable,
remarked, *that milord Anglois had admirable talents
for silence.*

Prodigality prevails in town, and economy in the
country, in more instances than may be at first imagined. In town, such is the number of newspapers,
that the coffee-house lounger may sate himself, like
a fly in a confectioner's shop, with an endless variety
of new sweets. He may see an event set in all possible lights, and may suit it to the complexion of his
mind, and the sentiments of his party. Such is the
advantage of a refined metropolis, where profusion
enlarges the dominions of pleasure in every direction,
and supplies the greatest dainties to gratify the vitiated appetite of curiosity. In the country, the case
is widely different. In most genteel families a solitary paper is introduced with the tea-urn and rolls,
but certain restraints are laid upon the manner of
perusing it: half the news is read the first morning,
and half is reserved for the entertainment of the next.
This frugal distribution in the parlour is, without
doubt, adopted from something similar which takes
place in the storeroom. The mistress of the family
dispenses the proper quantity of pickles and preserves,
and then locks the door till the following day. Our
affairs in the East are settled at one time; whilst the
burgomasters and the princess of Orange are left to
their fate till another. Enough is read to furnish the
family with subjects for conversation; and, as topics
are not numerous, the thread of politics is spun very
fine. Little miss wonders, when she hears papa ad-
just the affairs of the nation, that he is not a parlia-

ment man, and thinks that, if the king were ever to hear of him, he would certainly be made his prime minister.

There is (if the expression may be allowed) a refinement in our fears. A rational apprehension of impending evil is the mother of security, but the mind that is terrified by remote dangers is weak and ridiculous. The imagination is like a magnifying-glass, which, by enlarging the dimensions of distant objects, makes them appear formidable. It is the office of reason to place them in proper situations, and to suggest, that we are not exposed to their effects. The Neapolitan, who lives at the foot of Vesuvius, has just cause for trembling at the symptoms of an eruption; but, he may depend upon it, his vines are in no danger from the volcanos in the moon. The stockholder may well fear the consequences of the Belgic commotions. The farmer, whose hay is scattered over the meadows, may, without the imputation of weakness, be vexed at the torrents of rain. But why should the man, who has no concern but to walk from Cheapside to Whitechapel, apply to his barometer ten times before he ventures out; or be disturbed in his dreams for the safety of the grand signor?

A club was once established by certain gentlemen, whose minds were too much polished by their travels not to banish every thing that is interesting to John Bull. Among their rules and orders it was enacted, that no mention should be made of the state of the weather or politics, but that all their conversation should turn upon literature and virtue. It happened, that the president of the club, who was a pretty *petit maitre* of twenty stone, was attacked by a violent ague. He was seized with a cold fit whilst adjusting a dispute between two dilettanti, whether the church of Santa Maria in Navicelli was larger than Santa Maria in Valicelli. This important argument was interrupted by the president's digression in abuse of the English climate, which he declared was calculated for no beings under the sun but draymen and shepherds. Some of the fraternity talked peremptorily of expelling him from the society, for breaking their first rule, and introducing a subject which ought to be left to the canaille. After great animosity, and abundant altercation, it was finally determined to expunge the rule, because they could not engage a party who were sufficiently refined by liqueurs to be freed from the grievance of their English constitutions.

It was once seriously discussed by the French academy, whether it was possible for a German to be a wit. It would be more worthy of the sagacity of the same learned body to determine whether it be possible for an Englishman not to be a politician. To form a right decision, let them converse with what order of men they please, and they will find, that the ruling passion is the regulation of the political machine. The ferocity which is natural to islanders may be the reason of our being more disposed to command than to obey. Hence it is no uncommon case for a man so far to mistake his abilities, as to talk of riding the state horse, when he is hardly expert enough to shoe him. All persons of all ranks harangue as if the secrets of the state would be best intrusted to their discretion, as if their own address qualified them for the most critical situations, and the judgment of their rulers should be suspended until superior sagacity pointed out the right path. Whilst the barber snaps his fingers among his customers, he talks of managing the *mounseers*, and laying on taxes without oppression. The aldermen, at a corporation dinner, do the same over their turbot and venison. To complete the climax, these are the identical points which perplex the understandings of the king and his counsellors in the cabinet.

Notwithstanding the severity of military law, the different orders of society would sustain no injury, if, like a well-disciplined army, they neither broke their ranks, nor mutinied against their officers. A family is a kingdom in miniature: in that domestic, but important sphere of government, every man of common sense is able to preside. The master of a well-regulated house is more beneficial to the state, than a hundred political declaimers. To curb the passions, to fix religious principles in the minds of children, and to govern servants with mild authority, all ultimately promote the best interests of the public. Obedience branches out into various relations. The debt which we demand from our dependants, we owe to our governors. Subordination is to a subject, what resignation is to a Christian: they are both admirably well calculated to silence the clamours of party, and administer the cordial of content. Let the Englishman repress his murmurs, by reflecting that he is a member of a constitution which combines the excellences of all governments; and that he breathes in a climate which permits him to be exposed to the air more days in a year, and more hours in a day, without inconvenience, than any other in Europe.—Q.   KETT.

Nº 23.   SATURDAY, AUGUST 18, 1787.

Quadrupedante putrem sonitu quatit ungula campum.
VIRGIL.

AMONG the sources of those innumerable calamities which, from age to age, have overwhelmed mankind, may be reckoned, as one of the principal, the abuse of *words*. Dr. South has two admirable discourses on the subject; and it is much to be wished, that a continuation could be carried on, by some proper hand, enumerating the words, which, since his time, have successively come into vogue, and been, in like manner, abused to evil purposes, by crafty and designing men.

It is well known what strange work there has been in the world, under the name and pretence of *reformation*; how often it has turned out to be, in reality, *deformation*; or, at best, a tinkering sort of business, where, while one hole has been mended, two have been made.

I have my eye, at present, on an event of this kind, which took place in very early times, and is supposed to have been productive of many and great advantages to the species; I mean the alteration brought about in the ' economy of human walking;' when man, who, according to the best and ablest philosophers, went originally on four legs, first began to go upon two. I hope it will be excused, if I venture humbly to offer some reasons why I am led to doubt whether the alteration may have been attended by all the advantages so fondly imagined.

There is something suspicious in the history given of this reformation. It is said to have had the same origin with that ascribed by Dr. Mandeville to the moral virtues. It was the ' offspring of flattery, begot upon pride.' The philosophers discovered that man was proud : they attacked him in a cowardly manner, on his weak side, and by arguments, the sophism of which it might be easy enough, perhaps, if there were occasion, to unravel and expose, prevailed upon him to quit his primeval position ; and, whether fairly or not, they coaxed him upon two. How far any good is to be expected from a reformation founded on such principles, the reader must judge for himself.

By the account with which the authors of it have furnished us, thus much is certain, that nothing can be more unnatural : and yet, say these philosophers, at other times, ' Whatever you do, follow nature ;' a precept, which, in general, they seem very well disposed to practise, to the best of their abilities. A child naturally goes on all four ; and we know how difficult a matter it is to set him an end, or to keep him so. He has not even the stability of a ninepin, which will stand till it be bowled down. For my own part, I never see a child's forehead with a great bump upon it, or swathed up in a black-pudding, lest it should receive one, but I am irresistibly impelled to bewail this pretended reformation, as a most notorious and melancholy defection from our primitive condition.

When the two children brought up to man's estate, apart from all human beings, by the command of a king of Egypt, who imagined that the language which they should speak must necessarily be the original language of the world—when these children, I say, had the honour to be introduced at court, amidst a circle of all the learned, and wise, and noble personages of that celebrated country ; history bears her testimony, that they proceeded up the drawing-room, and made their way to the royal presence, upon *all four*. I am aware that some have thought they threw themselves into that attitude, from the dread and awe inspired into them by the sight of majesty ; others, still more refined, have supposed they might have done so, to adapt themselves to the employment of those whom they found assembled in that place, and be prepared either to creep, or to climb, or both, as opportunity offered. But I cannot apprehend, that the course of their education could have qualified them for speculations so abstruse as these; and, therefore, I must take leave to say, I look upon the fact to be good evidence, that such was the attitude proper to man.

I am still farther confirmed in my opinion, from that strong propensity visible in mankind, to return to it again. The posture, into which we have been seduced is productive of constant uneasiness. We are in a fidget from morning to night; to relieve us from which, the expense of chairs and sofas is a very considerable tax upon our property; and, after all, we cannot compose ourselves perfectly to rest, but when recumbent upon our beds. That our sole business is with earth, universal practice seems to determine. Why then should we look after any thing else? or why be reproached with *O curvæ in terras animæ?* especially when we recollect the fate of the poor astronomer, who, while he was gazing on the stars, fell into a ditch.

It deserves notice, that some of our most distinguished titles of honour are borrowed from our fellow-creatures, the quadrupeds, whose virtues we are ambitious to emulate. An accomplished young gentleman of family, fortune, and fashion, glories in the name, style, and title of a *buck*. You cannot pay him a greater compliment, than by bestowing on him this appellation; and indeed no one reason in the world can be assigned, why he should walk upon *two*.

The opinion of a great commercial nation like our own, cannot with more certainty be collected from any circumstance than from the management of the most important article of finance. Now, we find that article intrusted to the care of *bulls* and *bears*. And although a *bear*, which is a quadruped, by a metamorphosis no less sudden and surprising than any in Ovid, be at times transformed into a *duck*, which is a biped, yet it is observed, that there is a somewhat awkward about him ever after. He moves, indeed, but his motions are not as they should be, and he is from thenceforth said not to *walk*, but to *waddle*. It may be added, that we never hear of a duck commencing dancing-master; whereas Captain King informs us, ' the Kamtchadales are not only obliged to the *bears* for what little advancement they have hitherto made in the sciences or polite arts, as also the use of simples both internal and external ; but they acknowledge them likewise for their *dancing-masters*; the *bear-dance* among them being an exact counterpart of every attitude and gesture peculiar to this animal, through its various functions. And this dance is the foundation and groundwork of all their other dances, and what they value themselves most upon.'

I could have wished, that one of these Siberian teachers had been present the other day, to have bestowed a lecture upon a friend of mine, who had been instructed to marshal his feet in a tolerably decent way ; to move forward by advancing one before the other, and backward by sliding one behind another ; in short, he had attained some proficiency in what Dr. South styles, ' that whimsical manner of shaking the legs, called *dancing ;*' when, all at once, holding up his hands in an angle of forty-five degrees, with a countenance full of ineffable distress, and a most lamentable accent, he exclaimed to the master, ' But, Sir, what shall I do with *these ?*'

Nor is the complaint of my friend at all singular. For the truth is, (and why should I dissemble it ?) that since we have left off to put our arms to their due and proper use of fore-legs, they are ever in the way, and we know not what upon earth to do with them. Some let them dangle, at will, in a perpendicular line parallel with their sides ; some

fold them across their bosoms, to look free and
easy; some stick them a-kimbo, in defiance; some
are continually moving them up and down, and
throwing them about, so as to be at variance with
their legs, and every other part of their bodies;
as was the case with Dr. Johnson, when Lord Chesterfield had like to have fallen into a *deliquium* by
looking at him, and could consider the author of
the English dictionary in no other light than that
of an ill-taught posture-master. Some thrust their
hands, as far as they can, into their breeches pockets.
This last is a bad habit enough; because they who
find nothing in their own pockets (which, perhaps,
pretty generally happens), may be tempted to try
what they can find in those of others. While fore-
legs were in fashion, the limbs, which are now the
cause of so much embarrassment to us, had full employment: it might be said, ' Every man his own
horse :' and when one considers the present extravagant price of horses, one is induced on this account
also to wish that it had still continued to be so.

As I am upon the subject of the *reformations*
made in our persons, I cannot help mentioning a
little dab of one, effected in an age so distant, that
no system of chronology within my knowledge has
marked the era, much as it deserves to have been
marked. The period is altogether unknown, when
our nature was first despoiled of an appendage
equally useful and ornamental—I mean a *tail;* for,
with an eminently learned philosopher of North
Britain, I am most firmly persuaded, that it was
originally a part of our constitution ; and that, in
the eye of superior beings, man, when he lost that,
lost much of his dignity. If a conjecture might be
indulged upon the subject, (and, alas! what but
conjectures can we indulge?) I should be inclined
to suppose, that the defalcation, now under consi-

deration, was coeval with the change of posture discussed above. No sooner had man unadvisedly mounted on *two*, but his tail dropped off; or rather, perhaps, in the confusion occasioned by the change, it hitched in a wrong place, and became suspended from his head. But how very easy would it be, when the books are open, to make a transfer, and restore it to its proper situation? That very respectable person, whom Swift humorously described as ' lately come to town, and never seen *before* by any body,' has been known, upon some occasions, to have appeared in a tie-wig; which, doubtless, was his full dress, for balls and other public assemblies. But by way of light and airy morning dishabille, no one can doubt of his looking admirably well in a *queue*.

I am sensible this is a topic which requires to be treated with the utmost caution and delicacy; and, therefore, feeling the ground to tremble under me, I shall not venture to advance farther upon it; but from the disposition prevalent among us to copy the manners of creatures so much our inferiors, I shall conclude by encouraging my readers to hope the time cannot be very far distant, when we shall all have our *tails* again, and once more go upon *all four*.—Z.   BISHOP HORNE.

N° 24. SATURDAY, AUGUST 25, 1787.

Roscia, dic sodes, melior lex, an puerorum est
Nænia.—Hor.

' TO THE AUTHOR OF THE OLLA PODRIDA.

' IF all the qualities of the mind, or habits of life, which are found to be most adverse to religion, to

Christian virtue, and spiritual hope, were to be enumerated, a selfish sordid temper would not appear
the last upon the list. It is not intended by these
expressions, to point out, in gross terms, a base
avarice, a hardened churlish nature, or the disin-
genuous craft of men devoted to the world; but to
expose a disposition better covered from contempt,
recommended by careful instruction, and undeser-
vedly respected among men.

'We are in haste to withdraw the minds of the
young from wild and visionary notions of pleasure
and of life: it is better, indeed, to remove such notions prudently and seasonably, than to wait till disappointment snatches them away. Such gay romantic scenes as entertain them in the books they
read, such pleasing views of manners and of persons, elevated above the wants of life, its coarser
inconveniences, its sullen irksome hours, its attendant troubles and diseases, give but a false
draught of the state of man. These broken rays,
perhaps, of lost perfection, cannot, we know, penetrate far into the shades of life; they are the emanations of minds whose early purity is yet untainted
by the common ordinary objects and pursuits, the
passions and engagements of real life, disfigured as
it is. It is true, such views will soon be contradict-
ed by experience, by real images, by daily docu-
ments, by repeated and inevitable truth: but reason
should not assume too much applause in shaking off
these vain and empty notions; though she seem to
rise superior to them, she sinks, in fact, too often
much below them. The selfish reasoner and worldly
monitor, in banishing these phantoms, do not always
substitute more noble emulations; they pluck away
the weeds and the wild flowers, but they sow tares
at last. These are the men who fasten impudence
by precept upon honest natures; who rear and edu-

cate the baser passions of the heart, endear them by
familiar and popular names, point out their advantage, their expedience, and necessity: they chill the
warmth of untrammelled and disinterested minds;
they plunge themselves and others into selfish sordid
habits and opinions, in order to avoid the folly or
the inconvenience of those which are childish or
imaginary: they put away airy pleasures and speculations, to addict themselves to actual grossness.
But can we continue the dreams of fancy to the
ends of our lives? no more than we can the games
and amusements of children. The hand of experience will pluck away our soft and glittering robes;
the sun will vanish from our landscape; the leaves
drop from our shrubs: and we must learn to harden
ourselves against the true climate in which we are
to live.

'Some traces of delight from those fantastic images
of youth, remain for recollection; we acknowledge
them as true sources of pleasure, but we cannot recur to them. Reason compounds her judgments of
different materials: whatever is unnatural cannot
please or edify: it cannot please, because the sober
mind can only be interested by truth; it cannot
edify, because so little of it can apply to ourselves
or others. But the knowledge of these truths, as it
is applied by selfish and worldly men, does not improve the mind; it rather injures and contracts it.
The ridicule thrown upon false pleasures and ideal
amusements, leads the way to real sensuality: the
fear of being deluded and imposed upon, first abates
the warmth of true benevolence, and, at last, excuses churlishness and avarice. What, then, do
they gain too often by their boasted experience, by
their sagacity and emancipation, but suspicious
hearts, narrow minds, gross ideas instead of fanciful
ones, real errors, genuine arrogance, and substantial

ambition? There are men, indeed, who, under
cover of a kind of wisdom, secretly and indirectly
deride all eminent degrees of virtue as romantic and
impracticable : if you talk to them of pleasures or
of hopes, that do not meet the senses, they will turn
them into ridicule : if you speak to them of tenderness, of charity, and zeal, they will demonstrate
to you how unfit they are for the purposes of life.
But whether the juvenile and silly inexperience of
a warm imagination be well supplanted by the subsequent inveterate attachments, may be determined
by a closer estimate : and if it shall be found that
the real, the substantial, and immediate fruition,
so preferred, involves a paradox, is more a notion
than the other; deceives us more by universal testimony ; hurts us more ; is more a shadow ; more a
dream ; and has an issue infinitely worse, a sum of
covenanted ills, of woes ligitimate and permanent ;
there will be little scope remaining for complacency,
and still less expectation of better habits to succeed.

' If we shift only from the pleasures and chimeras
of imagination to the pursuits of appetite : if keen
desires, or real nakedness, succeed the sports and
masquerade of fancy; the change will not be flattering. It is matter rather of disgrace than gratulation,
that we are subject, in our chosen pleasures, to the
rule and the caprice of present things ; the fund and
objects of the senses.

' But to draw nearer to the mark and end of these
reflections—it is clear that such imaginary pursuits,
such wild and empty notions, as were first represented, such a temper of mind, occupied in fanciful
notions, will be found less abhorrent from what is
truly excellent, will be more easily converted into
right and lively impressions of what is really desirable and eminent, than that well-compacted, that

proud and sensual disposition, which is confirmed by solid enjoyment, such as it is, by the real fruits of worldly prudence, of temporal acquisitions, temporal gratifications, or temporal distinction. The wild conceits and speculations of the young disclose a taste for some superior kinds of pleasure, which is supported by the fancy before it finds a truer foundation—to point out that foundation, is the ultimate design of these remarks; that when the mind outgrows the thoughtless sports of childhood, or the ideal pageantries of youth, necessity or appetite may neither bend the neck to earth, nor furnish objects to keep up through life an easier chase, which leaves us weary when the day declines, ill repaid by exercise alone, or by a dead and worthless prize.

'To kindle in the soul a purer flame, whose radiance may dispel the glooms of life; to give the mind an object adequate to its sublimest scope and comprehension; to cherish regular and reasonable actions, calculated to an end consistent, absolute, and unequivocal; to preclude those blank and cheerless hours which harassed appetite and overworn invention, which disappointment or satiety, which uniformity or sullenness of temper, which the calms or clouds of life, must leave in those who terminate their views upon the present scene, who take new colours from the shifting hues of all things round them, and fluctuate on all their changes; to lift the heart, and raise the front of man—should be the care of tender relatives and skilful guides; of such as cannot but desire, that they, on whom they have entailed their weakness and their sorrows, should be partners, also, in their hopes on earth, and in their future glories.

'To furnish scenes analogous to those which fancy trod before, but opened to the steadfast eyes of reason and of hope, revealed to calm and salutary specu-

lation, and ensured in their reversion; to trace out
prospects far more ravishing than all the pages of
romance could feign, yet neither inaccessible nor
visionary, but properly and truly such as may concern and interest us, and may be our inheritance and
our portion : to keep the purest faculties, the noblest
energies of intellect, the powers and compass of the
soul, exalted and ascendant, elevated high above
the transient and embarrassed scene of temporal
vicissitudes and exigencies; should be the proper
aim of the philosopher, and is the great prerogative
of the   CHRISTIAN.'

POTT.

N° 25. SATURDAY, SEPTEMBER 1, 1787.

Decipimur specie.

THERE are, I believe, no paths of literature so be-
set with difficulties as definition and biography. Of
difficulties unsurmounted in biography we have
lamentable instances in those adventurers who have
attempted to write the life of Johnson; and the errors of definition are sufficiently apparent in those
who have laboured to instruct the world wherein consists true politeness.

From the writings of Lord Chesterfield, we collect, that politeness consists in the nameless trifles of
an easy carriage, an unembarrassed air, and a due
portion of supercilious effrontery. The attainment
of these perfections is the grand object to which the
son of many a fond and foolish parent is directed,
from whose conduct one might reasonably suppose
they thought every accomplishment, necessary or
ornamental to man, attainable through the medium

of the tailor, the hair-dresser, and the dancing-master; reserving only for the mind such salutary precepts as may tend to inspire pertness and insolent confidence.

In the Gelateo of the Archbishop of Benevento* are contained all the rules which are necessary to introduce a person into company, and to regulate his behaviour when introduced. Yet I cannot but think the plan of this, and every other treatise, too much confined, which would inform us, that it is the principal end of this qualification to fix the minutiæ of dress, and reduce manners to a system. He is supposed to have attained the summit of politeness, who can take an apparent interest in the concern of people for whom he has no regard; be earnest in inquiries after persons for whose welfare he is not solicitous; and discipline his bow, his smile, and his tongue, to all rules of studied grimace and agreeable insipidity. Thus, that politeness of which we hear so much, the race which every toothless dotard has run, and the goal to which every beardless fool is hastening, is only a hypocritical show of feelings we do not possess; an art by which we conciliate the favour of others to our own interest.—The two characters which are generally contrasted with each other, in order to shew the perfection of politeness, and the extreme of its opposite, are the soldier and the scholar; the former is exhibited to us with all the ornament of graceful manners and bodily accomplishments, with the advantages of early intercourse with the world, and the profit of observation from foreign travel. The advantages here enumerated, will, I fear, upon a nearer survey of them, appear visionary and unsubstantial, and not such as are likely in the end, to justify the hopes of those, who,

* Monsign. Giovanni de la Casa.

in the great love for their country, remove their sons
from school before they can have answered any end
for which they were sent thither; and produce them
to the world before they can have any fixed principle
to be the guide of their conduct. They make observations, of which ignorance and wonder are the
source; they form opinions in which judgment has
no share; they travel; and he who sets out a Mum-
mius is foolishly expected to return home a Cæsar.
In enumerating the disadvantages under which the
scholar labours, we are reminded, that a studious
and sedentary life are too apt to generate peevish
and morose habits, the bane of society, and the torment of their own possessor. We are told that the
student, receiving no impressions but such as books
are likely to make, cannot apply his observations to
the usage of common life; that he forms Utopian
opinions, and is surprised to find they cannot be
realized; that he becomes jealous of the dignity of
literature, for which the world seems to have too
little respect; and that the life which was begun
with the hopes of excelling in these pursuits wherein he finds few competitors, is at length concluded
in the disappointment of expected reputation, or the
scarce more sensible gratification of triumphs thinly
attended, and applauses partially given. In such
colours is the studious man painted to us, by our
arbiters of elegance, who, in their obliging zeal for
the regulation of our manners, confound learning
with pedantry; and, under pretence of removing
from us a trifling evil, would rob us of a substantial
good.

‘ Learning,’ says Shenstone, ‘ like money, may
be of so base a coin, as to be utterly void of use; or,
if sterling, may require good management to make it
serve the purposes of sense and happiness.’ What
Shenstone has here with truth affirmed *may* be, there

are others who have ventured with some confidence to declare *must* be.

True as it is, it would no doubt appear a paradox to many, should any one affirm, that the surest method of attaining politeness is to seek it through the medium of literature. We should have thought less of the politeness of Cæsar, but for the author of his Commentaries. Crichton would not have been called the mirror of politeness, merely for his skill in the tournament; nor would 'Granville the polite' have been the theme of Mr. Pope's song, for his address in entering a room. The truth is, we mistake a mental qualification for a bodily one. We expect politeness to be conveyed to us with our coat from the tailor, or that we may extract it from the heel of a dancing-master; when, in fact, it is only to be obtained by cultivating the understanding, and imbibing that sense of propriety in behaviour, with which the deportment of the body has, but at best, a secondary concern. I know not why it is, but from our misinterpretation of the word, that politeness, when applied to a virtuous action, immediately becomes ridiculous. Who would not suppose the chastity of the Roman general ironically commended, who should call that the politeness of Scipio, which others have called his continence?—Or would not the congregation of a grave divine be somewhat surprised to hear their preacher celebrating the politeness of the good Samaritan? Yet these acts are the substance of that virtue, to whose shadow we compliment away our rights and opinions, frequently our honesty, and sometimes our interests.

'Politeness,' says a good author of our own time, ' is nothing more than an elegant and concealed species of flattery, tending to put the person to whom it is addressed, in good humour and respect with himself.'

It is rather, in my opinion, the badge of an enlightened mind, and, if not a positive virtue in itself,
it is, at least, a testimony that its possessor has many
qualifications which are really such.—It lives in every
article of his conduct, and regulates his behaviour on
every occasion, not according to the whimsical and
capricious rules of fashion, but according to some
fixed principles of judgment and propriety. It prevents the impertinence of unseasonable joking, it re-
strains wit which might wound the feelings of another,
and conciliates favour, not by ' an elegant and concealed flattery,' but by a visible inclination to oblige,
which is dignified and undissembled. To the acquisition of this rare quality so much of enlightened
understanding is necessary, that I cannot but consider every book in every good science, which tends
to make us wiser, and of course better men, as a
treatise on a more enlarged system of politeness,
not excluding the experiments of Archimedes, or the elements of Euclid. It is a just observation of Shenstone, ' that a fool can neither eat, nor drink, nor
stand, nor walk, nor, in short, laugh, nor cry, nor
take snuff, like a man of sense.'   MONRO.

Nº 26. SATURDAY, SEPTEMBER 8, 1787.

WHEN I have had the good fortune to light upon
any subject which has been relished by the nice discerning palate of the public, it is my custom to try
whether something more cannot be made of it : for
having entered upon business with a moderate stock
only in trade, it is expedient for me to husband it
well, and to throw nothing away that can be used

again. Being born with an antipathy to plagiarism, *I will be free to confess* (as gentlemen express it in the house of commons), that I took the hint from my landlord of the Red Lion at Brentford; who, when some punch was called for, and there was no more fruit in the house, was overheard to say, in a gentle voice, to Mrs. Bonnyface, ' Betty, ca'sn't give the old lemons t'other squeeze ?'

I have demonstrated upon a former occasion—I should hope, to the satisfaction of every impartial person in Great Britain, the manifold advantages accruing to the community from the multiplication of newspapers among us. It has since occurred to me, that some directions might be given, as to the best method of reading a newspaper with profit and advantage. I mean not, whether it should be read longitudinally, latitudinally, or transversely ; though very great additions have been made to science by experiments of this kind ; but how it may be rendered productive of reflections in different ways, which will prove of real service in life.

I was not a little pleased, the other day, upon paying a visit at the house of a person of distinction in the country, to find the family assembled round a large table, covered with maps, and globes, and books, at the upper end of which sat a young lady, like a professor reading from the chair. In her hand she held a newspaper. Her father told me, he had long accustomed her, while reading one of those vehicles of intelligence, to acquaint herself with the several towns and countries mentioned, by turning to the names in Salmon's Gazetteer, and then finding them out upon the globe, or a map ; in which she was become so great a proficient, as to be at that time, in truth, giving a lecture in geography to her younger brothers and sisters. It was his farther intention, he said, ' that from Campbell's *Present State of*

Europe, she should acquire a sufficient knowledge of the history of the kingdoms around us, as well as our own, to form an idea of their importance and interests respectively, and the relation each bears to the rest.' Verily, thought I to myself, this is reading a newspaper to some purpose !

Children, very early in life, are eager for a sight of the newspaper. By being called upon, in a free and easy way, for some little account of what is in it, they may be gradually brought to read with attention, and to fix upon those articles which are most worthy of attention ; as also to remember what they have read, from one day to another, and put things together.

While we are in the world, we must converse with the world ; and the conversation, in part, will turn on the news of the day. It is the first subject we begin upon ; a general introduction to every thing else. All mankind, indeed, are our brethren, and we are interested, or ought to be interested, in their pleasures and their pains, their sufferings or their deliverances, throughout the world. Accounts of these should produce in us suitable emotions, which would tend to the exercise of different virtues, and the improvement of our tempers. We should accustom ourselves hereby to rejoice with those who do rejoice, and sympathize with those who mourn.

When any country is likely to become the theatre of remarkable events and revolutions (as, for instance, Holland, at this present moment), it is worth one's while to refresh one's memory with the history of that country, its constitution, and the changes it has heretofore undergone, the nature and disposition of the people, &c.—a sort of knowledge which is sure to be called for. The man who makes himself perfect and correct in it, will gain credit, and give pleasure, in every company into which it may happen to fall.

Whatever instruction is reaped from history, may be reaped from a newspaper, which is the history of the world for one day. It is the history of that world in which we now live, and with which we are, consequently, more concerned than with those which have passed away, and exist only in remembrance : though, to check us in our too fond love of it, we may consider, that the present, likewise, will soon be past, and take its place in the repositories of the dead.

There is a passage in the *Night Thoughts*, which I cannot resist the temptation of transcribing, as it contains one of the most astonishing flights of the human imagination, upon this awful and important subject, the transient nature of all sublunary things :

> Nor man alone : his breathing bust expires :
> His tomb is mortal. Empires die ; where, now,
> The Roman, Greek ? They stalk, an empty name !
> Yet few regard them in this useful light,
> Though half our learning is their epitaph.
> When down thy vale, unlock'd by midnight thought,
> That loves to wander in thy sunless realms,
> O Death ! I stretch my view ; what visions rise !
> What triumphs, toils imperial, arts divine,
> In wither'd laurels, glide before my sight !
> What lengths of far-famed ages, billow'd high
> With human agitation, roll along
> In unsubstantial images of air !
> The melancholy ghosts of dead renown,
> Whispering faint echoes of the world's applause,
> With penitential aspect, as they pass,
> All point at earth, and his at human pride,
> The wisdom of the wise, and prancings of the great.
>
> *Night*, ix.

Accounts of the most extraordinary events in old time are now perused by us with the utmost indifference. With equal indifference will the history of our own times be perused by our descendants ; and a day is coming, when all past transactions will appear in the same light, those only excepted, by a consideration of which we have been made wiser and better.

There are few, perhaps, by which we may not become so.

What nobler employment for the human mind, than to trace the designs of Providence in the rise and fall of empires; the overthrow of one, and the establishment of another upon its ruins! to watch diligently the different steps by which these changes are effected! to observe the proceedings of the great Ruler of the universe, always in strict conformity to the rules with which he himself has furnished us! to behold generals with their armies, and princes with their people, executing his counsels while pursuing their own! to view, upon the stage of the world, those scenes which are continually shifting, the different actors appearing in succession, and the gradual progress of the drama; each incident tending to develope the plot, and bring on the final catastrophe!

In the midst of these secular commotions, these conflicts of contending nations, it is useful to observe the effects produced by them on the state of religion upon the earth; while, among the powers of the world, some protect, and others persecute; some endeavour to maintain it in its old forms, and others wish to introduce new; all, perhaps, more or less, aim at converting it into an engine of state, to serve their own purposes, and to avail themselves of that influence which it must always have on the minds of men. Above and beyond these human machinations, a discerning eye sees the controlling power of heaven; religion preserved amidst the tumultuous fluctuations of politics; and the ark sailing in safety and security on the waters which threatened to overwhelm it.

When we read of the events taking place in our

own country, the subjects become more interesting, and we are in danger of having our passions roused and fomented. Let us, therefore, be upon our guard, judging of nothing by first reports, but awaiting the calmer hour of reason preparing to decide on full information. For the prosperity of our country let us be thankful and grateful; in its adversity, sorrowful and penitential; ever careful to correct our own faults before we censure those of others.

With respect to individuals and their concerns, examples (and they are not wanting among us) of piety, charity, generosity, and other virtues, should effectually stir us up to copy, to emulate, to surpass them; to join, so far as ability and opportunity will permit, in designs set on foot for the promotion of what is good, the discouragement and suppression of what is otherwise. And here there is great choice: many such designs are on foot; and let those, who have talents for it, bring forward more. All are wanted.

The follies, vices, and consequent miseries of multitudes, displayed in a newspaper, are so many admonitions and warnings, so many beacons, continually burning, to turn others from the rocks on which they have been shipwrecked. What more powerful dissuasive from suspicion, jealousy, and anger, than the story of one friend murdered by another in a duel? What caution likely to be more effectual against gambling and profligacy, than the mournful relation of an execution, or the fate of a despairing suicide? What finer lecture on the necessity of economy, than an auction of estates, houses, and furniture, at Skinner's or Christie's? —' Talk they of morals?' There is no need of Hutcheson, Smith, or Paley. Only take a newspaper, and consider it well; read it, and it will instruct thee, *plenius et melius Chrysippo et Crantore.*

A newspaper is, among other things, a register of mortality. Articles of this kind should excite in our minds reflections similar to those made by one of my predecessors, on a survey of the tombs in Westminster-abbey. They are so just, beautiful, and affecting, that my reader, I am sure, will esteem himself under an obligation to me, for bringing them again into his remembrance, by closing this paper with a citation of them :

‘When I look upon the tombs of the great, every emotion of envy dies in me ; when I read the epitaphs of the beautiful, every inordinate desire goes out : when I meet with the grief of parents upon a tomb-stone, my heart melts with compassion ; when I see the tomb of the parents themselves, I consider the vanity of grieving for those whom we must quickly follow : when I see kings lying by those who deposed them, when I consider rival wits placed side by side, or the holy men that divided the world with their contests and disputes, I reflect with sorrow and astonishment on the little competitions, factions, and debates of mankind. When I read the several dates of the tombs, of some that died yesterday, and some six hundred years ago, I consider that great day when we shall all of us be contemporaries, and make our appearance together.’*—Z.

BISHOP HORNE.

* Spectator, Vol. I. No. 26.

Nº 27. SATURDAY, SEPTEMBER 15, 1787.

> Mores hominum multorum videt et urbes.—HORACE.

> The grown boy, too tall for school,
> With travel finishes the fool.—GAY's Fables.

WE are informed by Plutarch, that Lycurgus forbade the Spartans from visiting other countries, from an apprehension that they would adopt foreign manners, relax their rigid discipline, and grow fond of a form of government different from their own. This law was the result of the most judicious policy, as the comparison made by a Spartan in the course of his travels would necessarily have produced disaffection to his country, and aversion to its establishments. It was, therefore, the design of the rigid legislator to confirm the prejudices of his subjects, and to cherish that intense flame of patriotism which afterward blazed out in the most renowned exploits.

So propitious is the British government to the rights of the people, so free is its constitution, and so mild are its laws, that the more intimate our acquaintance with foreign states is, the more reason we find to confirm our predilection for the place of our birth. Our legislature has no necessity, like that of the Spartan republic, to secure the obedience of its subjects by making ignorance an engine of state. But although England may rise superior in the comparison with foreign countries, it is much to be wished, that its pre-eminence was more frequently ascertained by cool heads and mature understandings; and that some check was given to the custom of sending youths abroad at too early an age. Innumerable instances could be adduced to prove, that, so far from any solid advantages being derived from the practice, it is generally pregnant with great and incurable evils. As soon as boys are emancipated from school, or have kept a few terms at the university, they are sent to ramble about the continent. The critical and highly improper age of nineteen or twenty is usually destined for this purpose. Their curiosity is eager and indiscriminate; their passions warm and impetuous; their judgment merely beginning to dawn, and of course inadequate to the just comparison between what they have left at home and what they observe abroad. It is vainly expected by their parents, that the authority of their tutors will restrain the sallies of their sons, and confine their attention to proper objects of improvement. But granting every tutor to be a Mentor, every pupil is not a Telemachus. The gaiety, the follies, and the voluptuousness of the continent address themselves in such captivating forms to the inclinations of youth, that they soon become deaf to the calls of admonition. No longer confined by the shackles of scholastic or parental restraint, they launch out at once into the wide ocean of fashionable indulgence. The only check which curbs the young gentleman with any force, is the father's threat to withhold the necessary remittances. The son, however, expostulates, with some plausibility, and represents that his style of living introduces him into the brilliant circles of the gay and great, among whom alone can be obtained the graces of polished behaviour, and the elegant attainments of genteel life. How much he has improved by such refined intercourse is evident on his return home. He can boast of having employed the most fashionable tailor at Paris, of intriguing with some celebrated madame, and appearing before the lieutenant de police for a drunken fray. He may, perhaps, more than once have lost his money at the ambassador's card parties, supped in the stables of Chantilli, and been introduced to the grand monarque at Versailles. The acquisitions he has made are such as must establish his character, among those who have never travelled, as a *virtuoso* and a *bon vivant*. By great good fortune he may have brought over a Paris watch, a counterfeit Corregio, and a hogshead of genuine Champagne. But it is well if his mind be not furnished with things more useless than those which he has collected for his pocket, his drawing-room, and his cellar. He has, perhaps, established a kind of commercial treaty with our polite neighbours, and has exchanged simplicity for artifice, candour for affectation, steadiness for frivolity, and principle for libertinism. If he has continued long among the votaries of fashion, gallantry and wit, he must be a perfect Grandison if he return not to his native country in manners a monkey, in attainments a sciolist, and in religion a sceptic.

From the expedition of some travellers, we are not to conclude, that knowledge of the world may be caught with a glance; or, in other words, that they are geniuses who 'grasp a system by intuition.' They might gain as much information if they skimmed over the continent with a balloon. The various places they fly through appear like the shifting scenes of a pantomime, which just catch the eye, and obliterate the faint impressions of each other. We are told of a noble Roman, who could recollect all the articles that had been purchased at an auction, and the names of the several buyers. The memory of our travellers ought to be of equal capacity and retentiveness, considering the short time they allow themselves for the inspection of curiosities.

The fact is, these birds of passage consult more for their fame than their improvement. To ride post through Europe is, in their opinion, an achievement of no small glory. Like Powel, the celebrated walker, their object is to go and return in the shortest time possible. It is not easy to determine how they can more profitably employ their whiffling activity than by commencing jockeys, expresses, or mail-coachmen.

Ignorance of the modern languages, and particularly the French, is a material obstacle against an Englishman's reaping the desired advantages from his travels. It is a common custom to postpone any application to them until a few months before the grand tour is commenced. The scholar vainly supposes that his own moderate diligence, and his master's compendious mode of teaching, will work wonders, by making him a complete linguist. From a slight knowledge of the customary forms of address, and a few detached words, the French language is supposed to be very easy. No allowance is made for the variety of the irregular verbs, the nice combination of particles, the peculiar turn of fashionable phrases, and the propriety of pronunciation. The great deficiencies in all these particulars are abundantly apparent as soon as *milord Anglois* lands on the other side of the channel. After venturing to tell his friends, to whom he has letters of recommendation, that he is *ravished* to see them, his conversation is at an end. His contracted brow, faultering tongue, and embarrassed air, discover that he labours with ideas which he wants words to express. Even the most just remarks, the most brilliant conceptions of wit, are smothered in their birth. To such a distressing case the observation of Horace will not apply—

Verbaque provisam rem non invita sequentur.

If he can arrive, after much stammering and hesitation, at the arrangement of a sentence, it abounds with such blunders and anglicisms as require all the politeness even of a Frenchman to excuse. Frequent attempts will, without doubt, produce fluency, and constant care will secure correctness; but the misfortune is, that the young traveller is employed by words, when his mind ought to be engaged with things. It is not less unseasonable than ridiculous, that he should be perplexing himself with the distinction between *femme sage* and *sage femme*, when he ought to be examining the theatre at Nîmes, or the canal at Languedoc.

Ignorance of the languages is a great inducement to the English to associate together when abroad. The misfortune of this practice is, that they spend their time in poisoning each other's minds with prejudices against foreigners of whom they know little from personal experience, and of whom they have not the laudable ambition of knowing more. Their more active employments consist in such diversion as they have transplanted from home. They game, play at cricket, and ride races. The Frenchman grins a contemptuous smile at these exhibitions; and shrewdly remarks, that Monsieur John Bull travels more to divert him than to improve himself. Rather than give occasion for this ridicule, our young gentlemen had better remain at home, upon their paternal estates, and collect their knowledge of other countries from Brydone's Tour, Moore's Travels, or Kearsley's Guides.—Q.

KETT.

Nº 28.   SATURDAY, SEPTEMBER 22, 1787.

> ——— When I did hear
> The motley fool thus moral on the time,
> My lungs began to crow like chanticleer,
> That fools should be so deep contemplative ;
> And I did laugh, sans intermission,
> An hour by his dial.—SHAKSPEARE.

‘ TO THE AUTHOR OF THE OLLA PODRIDA.

‘ SIR,

‘ MANY people indulge themselves in the too frequent introduction of what they are pleased to call moral sentiment into their conversation. Whilst they are thus endeavouring, by the trite precepts of dull and sententious gravity, to inculcate the lessons of virtue, they oftentimes put common sense to the blush, and generally make that ridiculous which they wish should appear amiable. I shall endeavour to illustrate my observation, by presenting you with a short sketch of a relation, with whom, as a boy of sixteen, in the intervals of school vacation, I have occasionally spent a week or two.

‘ Mr. Solomon Hatchpenny is an uncle of mine, who being most part of the week a tobacconist in the Borough, is on Saturday and Sunday a country gentleman, dwelling four miles from London. He is a very good sort of man, goes to church every Sunday, where he shuts his eyes, but declares he never sleeps ; has three wigs, pays every one his own, and keeps a four-wheel chaise. His country-house, which has been greatly improved since he bought it, by the addition of a bow window and a bench, stands within three yards of the road ; and, as he is unwilling to display less grandeur than his neighbours, he has laid out his ground, consisting of a garden of forty-four square feet, with that taste by which the family of the Hatchpennys has ever been distinguished. It contains a basin with the usual compliment of two artificial swans (which my uncle assures me when he bought them were as white as alabaster) and a gravel walk, each end of which is guarded by a pasteboard grenadier. In the middle of his walk is a dial, from which the morning sun is excluded by the grenadier's cap; and upon his house are three weathercocks, each pointing a different way. He generally takes an opportunity to prove to his guests, that his sentinels are as exact representations of live soldiers as can come from the hands of a painter and glazier, by informing them, that a sparrow having settled on the shoulder of one of them, he heard a child, who on passing, exclaimed, "Look, mamma, the corporal has caught a bird." This circumstance is to Mr. Hatchpenny a source of heartfelt satisfaction: he attributes the mistake of the child to his own skill in furnishing the deceit. He is pleased with the idea that he has given proof of his understanding in the very instance which declares his want of it. He is an example of happiness arising from ignorance, which, contrary to the lot of every other species of happiness, no man envies in another, and no man wishes for himself. Excuse my observations, and permit me to proceed. I am informed that my uncle Solomon is a politician at the club, and amongst his neighbours a wit; that he has been known to utter shrewd jokes upon the ministry, to quote profane rhymes from Poor Robin's Almanack, and to indulge himself in all those fanciful relaxations of the mind to which every good citizen is entitled, not inconsistent with his trade, his understanding, or his taste. It is, however, his peculiar study to hide every little sally of his wit from my observation, and confine all conversation uttered within my hearing to morality ; the essence of which, according to his opinion, consists in gravity and a long face. This gravity I never knew my uncle relax but once, and then it was in order to tell me, that a gentleman, who came to solicit his vote for a lectureship in the Borough, had absolutely won him over from an opposite party by paying a pretty compliment to his country-box, which he was pleased to denominate *Tully's Tusculum.* I took that opportunity of making an attempt (an awkward one, I suppose, because it was not understood) to pay the same kind of pretty compliment to his tobacco warehouses, which I begged leave to christen *Tully's Offices.* My uncle and I sometimes traverse what he calls his *premises,* which, without much bodily exertion, may be accomplished in something less than four minutes and a half, but according to our plan of proceeding, it generally consumes near an hour. The leaden swans (which, by a very classical metamorphosis, are now become black) are the innocent causes of much impatience to me : they delay us in our journey round the premises, while they furnish my uncle with an opportunity to display his discoveries in morality, and to descant upon the rapid flight of time : " Not seven years ago," says he, " till next twenty-fourth of July, did I buy those birds of Mr. William Dreadnought, plumber, in Fenchurch-street. They were then as pretty bits of fowl as ever were turned out of a shop. Learn from this, nephew, that the strongest things will decay : and consider the rate at which time passes." " Yes, Sir, sixty minutes to the hour, twelve hours to the day, and twelve months to the year."—" Right, nephew, calendar months." It was settled calendar months, and we proceeded. The weathercocks only delayed us while we observed that they were happily emblematical of the mutability of human events ; that one of them wanted greasing, and that a high station was no exemption from the inconveniences and wants of life. We now reached the gravel-walk, where I ventured, with all the gravity of speech and countenance I could summon, to hint my doubts as to the propriety of his having fixed up in his garden two objects which might possibly deceive some people into an opinion that they were men, when in fact they were not so. But, to qualify my observation, I thought it prudent to throw in something which he might understand as a compliment, and induce him to open his whole mind upon so momentous a subject. I told him that a petty tradesman might please himself in deceptions of that kind, without the danger of misleading any one ; but that I thought it rather improper in him, to whose motions the world turned the eye of observation, who had been known never to refuse the payment of a bill at sight, who had never indulged himself beyond a Chelsea bun, and a glass of Herefordshire cider on a Sunday, and who was undoubtedly the first tobacconist in the whole street. I saw my uncle was pleased with my argument: he attempted rather to excuse than defend what he had done. He confessed it was a deceit, yet he hoped a harmless one ; that when he was younger than he now is, he had sacrificed something to taste ; he remembered, to say the truth, when he first put them up, that his conscience rather misgave him ; but, to quiet his apprehensions, he had written upon each of their gunlocks, *To prevent mistakes, these are not real men, but only sham ones.*—W. D. fecit.

' I was fully satisfied with a subject on which whatever arguments I might have conceived, my countenance would not suffer me to declare.

' I left the house of this moral philosopher a few days ago with many good injunctions, which he who remembers may at least be entertained, if not edified. In the last conference which I enjoyed with him, he delivered himself to me in something like the following words :—" My dear nephew, I have your interest very much at heart, and should be glad to see you as well in the world as myself. You are certainly much improved, and can now, I dare say, have a just value for a few maxims which I shall lay down for the regulation of your conduct. Trust me, I know a little of these matters; old heads, and old shoulders; and though I say it that shouldn't say it, I can tell a six from a nine as well as those that make such a flourish with their wise pates and empty pockets. With regard to your studies, your master can probably direct you as well as I can; I only advise you, above all things don't puzzle your brains and waste your labour in writing verses. I never knew a fellow that had a shilling in his pocket write verses : you may as well expect to pick up gold under the pump at Aldgate as to get any thing by it. I caution you against reading novels and elegies, and all bad books. There is a book I have heard, which pretends to prove that there is no such thing as time : but this is all a flam, and I tell you there is, and very precious it is. He who loses it had better lose his dinner; and to him who makes the most of it 'tis as money in the stocks. There's a little money for you : go, and mind your book, and don't ride jackasses on Sundays; for the poor beasts should have a day's rest, and you'll only tear your best breeches, and incur the displeasure of your master."

' I shall here finish my account of Mr. Hatchpenny, only informing you, that he is a married man; and, should the patience of your readers not be quite exhausted, I shall take some opportunity

of giving you a little insight into the character of
my aunt. She is not a moralist of the same kind
exactly as her husband, and will not therefore afford
an example of the same species of folly. They shine
in different spheres, and are upon most considera-
tions better asunder. Tell your readers, if you
please, lest they should not have observed it, that
the dull solemnity of proverbial wisdom, which consists in " shreds of sentences," and remnants of
moral sayings, being applicable to all occasions, and
accessible to all understandings, is no proof of wisdom or honesty. And let those who are satisfied
with such kind of knowledge, improve their system,
by adding to it some excellent treatises from the repository of Mr. Newberry, adapted to the meanest
capacities, " price twopence halfpenny, adorned with
cuts."   I am, Sir, yours, &c.

SOCRATES IN EMBRYO.'

MONRO.

N° 29. SATURDAY, SEPTEMBER 29, 1787.

—— Ridiculum acri
Fortius et melius plerumque secat res.—HOR.

IT is wisely ordained by the laws of England, that
' the person of the monarch is sacred ;' as also that
' the king can do no wrong.' The meaning of this
last maxim I take to be, that, if wrong should happen
at any time to be done, the blame is to be laid upon
the administration, and not upon the king.

A friend, some years ago, took me into the House
of Commons, to attend the debates upon the opening
of a session; when an honourable gentleman made
so free with the speech, which I had but just before

heard most gracefully pronounced by his Majesty from the throne, that my hair stood an end, and I was all over in a cold sweat; till, towards the close of his oration, he relieved and restored me, by mentioning, in a parenthesis, that the speech was always considered, in that assembly, as the speech of the *minister*.

Sheltering myself, therefore, under this distinction, I cannot refrain from offering a few remarks on a late production, pregnant, as many are of opinion, with much mischief to the community. The reader sees that I mean, 'A Proclamation for the encouragement of piety and virtue, and for preventing and punishing of vice, profaneness, and immorality.' That the scheme proposed should be carried into execution, does not, indeed, seem probable. When we consider how long vice, profaneness, and immorality have been increasing among us, what a powerful party they have formed, how much fashion is on their side, and how very strong the tide runs, the attempt may be thought to resemble that of the man, who endeavoured to stop the Thames at London-bridge with his hat, unless the rich and the great would set the example.

I have always been an enemy to pains and penalties. The word *punishment* is a bad word, and the thing itself is much worse. When once it begins, the wisest man living cannot tell where it will end, or what will become of our liberties: for as the sheep-stealer said, 'If a gentleman cannot kill his own mutton, without being hanged for it, I should be glad to know what we have got by the revolution.' In short, one must be without a nose, not to smell something here of arbitrary power.

The idea of a Sunday, unenlivened by a little innocent play, is a very dull and dreary one. I know a family in town that has made the experiment. The consequence was, that before nine in the evening, the members of it found themselves so cross, peevish, and out of temper, that had it not been for an early supper and a glass of good wine, they could not have gone to bed in Christian charity with each other.

But much more distressful still was the case of a lady, whose husband, being in the commission, had lent his assistance to suppress gaming on a Sunday in a neighbouring public-house. It struck him that cards on that day, in a private house, might not, just then, be quite so proper ; and he ventured to hint as much to his lady. She had always apprehended the Gospel to have been designed for the *poor;* and was astonished to find that any thing in the proclamation could apply to persons of her rank in life. ' The party was made, and what could be done ?' A thought, however, luckily occurred ; and when the company was assembled, after an apology suitable to the occasion, instead of the card-tables, she introduced the entertainment of *catches and glees.* The thing took mightily, and was judged a pretty variety. Otherwise, a disappointment of such a nature, spreading, as it must have done, like an electrical shock, through all the polite circles, might have bred bad blood, and produced a general insurrection.

It fares with religion as with a shuttlecock, which is stricken from one to another, and rests with none. The rich apprehend it to have been designed for the poor ; and the poor, in their turn, think it calculated chiefly for the rich. An old acquaintance of mine, who omitted no opportunity of doing good, discoursed with the barber who shaved him, on his manner of spending the Sabbath (which was not quite as it should be), and the necessity of his having more religion than at present he seemed to be possessed of. The barber, proceeding in his work of lathering, replied, ' that he thought he had tolerably well for a barber; as, in his apprehension, one-third of the religion necessary to save a gentleman, would do to save a barber.'

I mention this, because I have received a letter of considerable length, praying redress of grievances, from a person who lets lodgings in Broad St. Giles's. He speaks of a very snug and comfortable neighbourhood there, which is likely to be broken up and dispersed by the proclamation, and nobody can well tell why.

He himself holds twenty houses by lease, which are let out, ready furnished. Matters are conducted in a manner so perfectly economical, that though there is no more than one bed in each room, there are usually two or three, and sometimes even four occupiers of that one room and bed. That the furniture is of an expensive and luxurious kind, no one can say; as it consists only of a stump bedstead, a flock bed, a pair of sheets (frequently only one sheet), a blanket or two, a chair or two (generally without backs), and a grate, but mostly without shovel, tongs, and poker. The sheets are usually marked with the name of the owner; and the words 'stop thief!' are added, for private reasons.

In two adjoining allies are forty more houses, let out in like sort to inhabitants, in number 400, consisting of whores, pickpockets, footpads, housebreakers, and thieves of every description, from all quarters of the town. But what then? They must have lodgings as well as other people; and, if they were to be in the street all night, it would be dangerous for the rest of his Majesty's subjects to pass. To avoid suspicion, the houses are continually lighted, and kept open all night; and to shew that hypocrisy has no place there, what used to be practised only in private at midnight, is now practised in public at mid-day.

To accommodate the poor, there are twopenny lodging-houses. One man, in particular, makes up, every night, thirty-five beds, and takes in men and women, at twopence or threepence a night; but if a man and woman comes in together, he receives one shilling a night for the two.

No society can be under better regulations than this is. Thus, for instance, when a prostitute has decoyed a man, and robbed him, the mistress of the house has half the pay and the plunder; and if one of these ladies intrude upon that beat, and walk, which another regards as her *exclusive right*, the matter is determined, as much greater matters are, by a *battle*.

Nor can there be reason to fear, that this society should ever become so numerous, as to be any annoyance to the public; since care is taken, that a sufficient number is hanged every session, to maintain a balance; and some rooms are always reserved for the reception of the dead bodies, which are brought back, after execution, to their old lodgings, till they can be otherwise disposed of.

Such is the substance of my friend's letter, which he desires may be communicated, through the channel of my paper, to his countrymen, that they may know what they have to expect from the present system of despotism; when a few neighbours cannot live peaceably together, without being disturbed and hunted out by proclamations. He hopes all honest men will join with him in a petition for ' the removal of evil counsellors;' and concludes with the old British axiom, ' My house is my castle;' under no dread, as it should seem, of the retort courteous once made to such a declaration by a magistrate in Oxford, of arbitrary principles; ' Then, Sir, the castle shall be your house.'

It is not easy to estimate the loss which the community at large will sustain by the dissolution of this worthy neighbourhood. For if a gentleman be robbed of his watch, it must be replaced by another: if his portmanteau be stolen, he must buy new clothes and linen: if his house be broken open, and stripped of its furniture, he must apply to the upholsterer: if he be beaten and wounded, to the surgeon: nay, should he be even killed, the undertaker and the sexton will be the better for it: and if the usual quantity of gin be not consumed, ruin must seize on those who vend it. Trade must stagnate. Thus incontrovertibly doth it appear, that private vices (if, indeed, they may be called vices) are public benefits.

I say, ' if they may be called vices;' because I do not see why, should we so please, they may not be called virtues. The nature of things, in themselves, is nothing; our opinion of them is all: and if our opinion alters, the names of things should alter with it: indeed, they do, and must do so. Thus, when two gentlemen go out with pistols, and shoot each other through the head or the heart, it is no more than ' an affair of honour:' when one seduces the wife or the daughter of another, it is merely an ' attachment:' and to cheat a man out of his estate, is only to ' pluck a pigeon.' In the neighbourhood above described, the nomenclature is much farther advanced, and has nearly attained perfection. They have a language peculiar to themselves, in which, when they relate their transactions, they may have been doing what is perfectly just and right for any thing we can tell to the contrary, since the words are not to be found in any dictionary but their own.

Here then, as some will think, is a more expeditious way of preventing vice, than by proclamation;

and, what is much to be desired, of doing it without infliction of punishment, by the sole and simple expedient of voting vice to be virtue.

The scheme is plausible; but, I must confess, I have my doubts. If we once vote vice to be virtue, I am afraid, that, by a necessity of nature, virtue, *per contra*, must become vice; and so we shall but be where we were: there will still be vice in the world.

When the welfare of his country is concerned, every man loves to be a little bit of a projector. On going deeper into the subject, I think I have hit upon a plan, which will make root and branch work of it, and do the business effectually.

That the effect may cease, the cause must be removed. Now, what is the cause of vice? Most undoubtedly, the *law:* for, were there no law, there could be no transgression. Abolish then, at once, the use of all law, human and divine. I grant the step a bold one, requiring a minister of firmness and resolution to take it; but when once taken, the advantages will be many and great.

In the first place, vice will, at one stroke, be extirpated from the face of the earth; for when a man has no law but his own will, we may defy him to do any thing illegal. Never trust to moral impossibility, where physical is to be had.

Secondly, it will put an end to the expense and trouble of law-suits; and (as equity would fall with law) to all tedious and everlasting suits in chancery, so much and so long complained of.

Thirdly, it will be a saving to the nation of one-tenth of the produce of all the lands in England and Ireland; and, consequently, put a stop to the ravages of the White-boys and Right-boys in this latter kingdom, as well as all disputes between ministers and their parishioners, in the former; since, as there would be no more occasion for reading prayers and preaching, the payment of tithes must, of course, be at an end.

Fourthly, it will procure a perpetual holyday for the gentlemen of either robe, who, in future, will have nothing to do, but to hunt, shoot, and play at cards. The same may be said respecting the members of both houses of parliament.

Fifthly, it will make Sunday as cheerful a day as any day of the week.

Lastly, it will remove all odium from the magistrates who have granted a licence to the Dog and Duck.

Such are the conveniences that would attend the execution of my plan; and after considering the subject on all sides, for six hours, in my elbow-chair, I protest, I cannot think of any one inconvenience to set against them; nor can I devise any method likely to be so effectual in redressing the grievances occasioned by the proclamation to the subject.

It remains only, that I mention one, which may possibly be occasioned by it to the crown; and which, indeed, I might not have thought of, but for the visit paid me, as I was closing this paper, by an honest farmer. ' So, Robin,' said I to him, ' rare news from London. The king is to be served now only by good and virtuous courtiers!'—' Ah, Lord have mercy upon me, Sir!' replied Robin; ' God bless his majesty, and grant him long to reign! But I am afraid as how he will be sometimes obliged to *help himself.*'—Z.

BISHOP HORNE.

N° 30.　SATURDAY, OCTOBER 6, 1787.

*Difficilis, querulus.—*Hor.

'My good Sir—What is your name? Your English name, I mean; for neither I, nor the parson of our parish, know what to make of your *Olla Podrida.* If it were Latin, Greek, or Hebrew, the doctor says he could give a good account of it: but you Oxford and Cambridge wits (especially the latter) have lately got a habit of introducing half a page of Italian, French, or Spanish (untranslated), into your works, though it is five hundred to one, not one in five hundred understands these languages. Well; but this *Olla Podrida*—my wife thinks it means a powdering-tub, in which tongues or hams, beef and pork, are salted and preserved against Christmas; as letters and essays, wise sayings and apophthegms, sprinkled with your Attic salt, are preserved in your miscellany for our winter evenings' amusement. This, however, is my first complaint; " That I do not know what to make of the title of your work."

' My second subject of complaint is this : my grandson, who is at the university, and is your acquaintance, sent me word that there was a new *paper,* lately come out, which every body reads; and, as a paper, now-a-days, means a newspaper, I desired him to send it me down; but what was my disappointment, when I found not a word of news in it ! Not a robbery or a murder; not a forgery, a rape, or an elopement; nor, what I more wished for, not a letter or even a paragraph to abuse the ministry; to reprobate the commutation-tax or the commercial treaty ; nor any prophetic calculation to soothe my fancy; to demonstrate the desperate state of this devoted nation, and prove that we are tottering on the verge of annihilation. This, I say, is the object of my second complaint.

' But, thirdly, as your paper reaches us on a Monday morning, I comforted myself, at best, with the hopes of entertaining my wife and daughter with something cheerful and facetious, after a rigid and gloomy observance of the sabbath, in consequence of his majesty's proclamation (for we have now no card-assembly at our house; only half-a-dozen old ladies who join us at tea, and take a solemn retrospect of every sin and transgression which their neighbours, not themselves, have been guilty of the preceding week)—But even in this hope I was frustrated; for I had just put on my spectacles, and read a few lines in your paper, when the excessive poignancy of your wit [*Here my modesty obliges me to omit a few words of compliment.*]

' This, then, is my third, but not my last complaint; for complaining and grumbling is the only comfort I have in this world; and this, Sir, though a very old and trite topic, is the subject of this letter. My reasons for troubling you I will beg leave to explain.

' My grandson, whom I mentioned, spent a good part of his puerile years under my roof; and has taken it into his head that I am a very learned man (though I never had a learned education), from a custom I have got of retiring from my family, many hours in the day, to my study, where I was always found, when called to dinner, with a great folio before me; and at the instant any one came to the door, I was just then turning over my leaf; and, as if I were in the midst of my subject, told them I would come immediately, and ordered them to sit down to dinner. This had the air of a profound student and deep meditation; when, perhaps, I was only weighing my guineas, calculating my interest money or my next half-year's rent; or, at best, conning over some of the opposition papers (every one of which I take in) as food for my querulous disposition.

'As I am unwilling, however, to discover to my family that I made no use of my pompous library, and read nothing but newspapers; and to oblige my grandson aforesaid, I have sent you a paragraph from an old author, in folio, well known in his day, which graphically describes the disease (for I am conscious it is a disease) under which I myself and many of my neighbours labour—that of grumbling and complaining, from morning till night, from mere habit and indulgence, or for want of something else to say.

'The most important subject of our complaint, is the state of public affairs; for which, perhaps, there may be some reason: but, though I have lived threescore years in the world (from the days of Sir Robert Walpole to Mr. Pitt's administration), I never knew it otherwise.

'I have been settled these thirty years on my estate in the country; but neither I nor my tenant, in all that space of time, have experienced one fruitful season, or hardly one seasonable day. We have been plagued with too much rain or too much dry weather: sometimes the frost has been too severe; sometimes the winter too mild, and the corn too rank—In a bad harvest we dreaded a famine—In a plentiful year we expected to be ruined by the low price of grain.

'I go to the coffee-house at our next market-town —I hear the same grumbling and complaints. In the winter, "Bless me, Sir, how could you ride over the Down this cold wind?" In summer, "Are not you melted with heat, or choked with dust?" In autumn, " I am told it is a nasty fog." In the spring, " The north-east winds will be the death of us." Thus that beautiful variety, which nature has so wisely contrived for the benefit of the whole creation, is made the constant subject of murmuring and discontent.

' I have a very good neighbour, who is an invalid; he has a small pudding made for himself, by a particular receipt, every day of his life: I frequently dine with him; he grumbles the whole dinner time about his pudding, but he eats it all; and his wife tells me he has done the same these seven years; but she never knew him leave a morsel of his pudding for the children.

' If you were to see us with one or two more of our sociable neighbours, over a bowl of punch, or a tankard of ale, you would compare us to the children of Israel, weeping by the waters of Babylon, in their captivity—such a shaking of the head, and lifting up of hands! such gloomy presages, and dismal inuendos! " Well, I say nothing, but if this weather continues, God send we may be all alive this day three months!"

' But every one must see daily instances of such people, who complain from a mere habit of complaining; and make their friends uneasy, and strangers merry, by murmuring at evils that do not exist, and repining at grievances which they do not really feel.

' But this is sufficient to introduce the character which I mentioned, drawn by Bishop Hall; and which proves, that the same evil has existed from the days of Solomon, King of Israel, to those of one who fancied himself as wise as Solomon, James the First, King of England—" It is naught, it is naught, saith the buyer; but when he is gone away, then he boasteth." Thus it was in the days of Solomon : in James's reign, Dr. Joseph Hall gives this account of " The Malcontent."

' " He is neither well, full nor fasting : and though he abound with complaints, yet nothing dislikes him but the present ; for what he condemns while it *was*, once past, he magnifies and strives to recall it out of the jaws of time. What he hath he seeth not, his eyes are so taken up with what he wants ; and what he sees, he careth not for, because he cares so much for that which is not.

' " When his friend carves him the best morsel, he murmurs, ' that it is an happy feast wherein each one may cut for himself.' When a present is sent him, he asks, ' Is this all ? And what no better !' and so accepts it, as if he would have his friend know how much he is bound to him for vouchsafing to receive it.

' " It is hard to entertain him with a proportionable gift. If nothing, he cries out of thankfulness ; if little, that he is basely regarded ; if much, he exclaims of flattery, and expectation of a large requital. Every blessing hath something to disparage and distaste it : children bring cares ; single life is wild and solitary ; eminence is envious, retiredness obscure, wealth burdensome, mediocrity contemptible. He never is tied to esteem or pronounce according to reason. Some things he must dislike, he knows not wherefore, but he likes them not ; and sometimes, rather than not censure, he will accuse a man of virtue. Every thing he meddleth with he either *findeth* imperfect or *maketh* so."

I am, Sir, yours, &c.

B.'

GRAVES.

Nᵒ 31. SATURDAY, OCOBER 13, 1787.

*Ubi per socordiam, vires, tempus, ingenium, defluxêre, na-
turæ infirmitas accusatur.*—SALLUST.

IT is the common topic of complaint among moralists, that mankind is a vain and idle race ; that we
aim at attainment for the enjoyment of which our
nature has not qualified us ; and that we suffer those
abilities which are entrusted to us, to be frittered
away in mean employments, or to be eaten up by the
rust of idleness.   It is thus, that in general denun-
ciations against human depravity, all persons at
times indulge themselves ; some gratify their pride
by noticing the frequency of those failings, from
which they consider themselves as exempt ; and
others find an opportunity of excusing their favourite follies, by placing those frailties to the account of
human weakness, which are due to their wilful neglect of right, or their headstrong perseverance in
error.   They make little haste to repent of those
crimes, in the participation of which they see mankind so universally engaged, and fondly imagine
that, in the general defection from virtue, the frailties
of an individual are of small account.   While we
are thus willing to impose upon ourselves, apolo-
gizing for our vices by arguments which only prove
the general tendency to be vicious, every man con-
tributes something to the increase of that evil, of
whose bulk and growth every man continues to complain.

Successfully have the labours of those wise men
been expended, who, by their zeal for the welfare of
mankind, and their accurate knowledge of human
nature, have been able to furnish the world with pre-

cepts of morality, which from their brevity are easily committed to memory, and from their good sense and propriety convey their meaning to the minds of the most unenlightened. The lessons they have left are intended to instruct us in the duties we owe to religion and society; to excite us to virtue by stigmatizing vice; and to check the pride of man, by reminding him of his limited capacity. Yet the benefits thus conferred upon us are too frequently abused by cunning and designing men. The arguments which were intended to restrain extravagance, are wielded for the defence of covetousness, and each extreme of vice excuses itself by attacking its opposite. The son of avarice, thriving in his misery, has abundance of maxims, which he pours forth without relenting upon the votaries of heedless gaiety and unfruitful dissipation, who are content, in return, with urging the insufficiency of wealth, and the folly of those who seek it. Various are the apophthegms by which philosophy is enabled to condemn ignorance; and ignorance is quite satisfied with itself in ridiculing the vanity of human wisdom.

An attempt has lately been made to rescue the lower orders of people from their extreme of ignorance, by the appropriating one day in the week to the instilling of religious knowledge into the minds of the young, and exciting in them a desire of intellectual improvement. For the prosecution of this plan, sermons have been preached, subscriptions opened, and every mode of persuasion and encouragement been adopted, that wealth, learning, and benevolence could suggest. Yet to these laudable designs there have been found many enemies. Armed with the fallacies of logic, they have with sufficient ingenuity demonstrated to us, that the ignorance of the multitude is a public good; that to the 'hewers of wood, and drawers of water,' learning is injurious or unprofitable; and that the husbandman and the mechanic have other objects on which their attention is more properly engaged than wisdom and science. All the arguments which were first produced to restrain the arrogance of the overwise, are made use of to reconcile ignorance to its darkness, and to hide the light from those, who, having never enjoyed it, are little solicitous to acquire what they have so long been able to live without. Many of these reasoners have answered some private end. Some have discovered the skill with which they can argue in a bad cause; and others, under the sanction of such reasoning, have indulged their avarice, by sparing their money. But let him who would prove that ignorance is either a blessing or a virtue, remember, that he advances the position of a wicked man, which he must support with the arguments of a fool. The same reason which informs us, that to make such an attempt is unjust, adds the comfortable assurance, that to succeed in it is impossible.

There is, perhaps, some cause of complaint against the people themselves; who appear too little anxious for their own welfare, who neglect to catch the opportunity which presents itself of emerging from their darkness, and by their inattention thwart the designs of those who interest themselves in their behalf, or render the success of them partial and limited. There is, I believe, in the minds of the lower class, an almost universal prevalence of inclination to receive instruction from one of their own order. They choose rather to deal with the same person for their cabbage-nets and their Christianity, their pickled pork and their prayers, than receive their religious information from the hands of him whom learning has made more able to inform them, and who is more likely to be honest, if it be only that he has less temptation to be otherwise. They have no value for what they do not understand, and no inclination to understand what those have taught them is unprofitable, whose interest it is to flatter their ignorance and indulge their prejudices.

There are many persons whom betrayed confidence or disappointed expectation have driven from the world, to indulge in private their ill-founded resentment against the sons of men. They leave the haunts and ' the busy hum of men,' to brood in solitude over their discontents; they continue to live in the studious and constant neglect of the duties they owe to society, and endeavour, by perseverance, to persuade themselves they can despise mankind. Not unfrequently to this compound of wickedness and folly do they give the title of philosophy. It is the peculiar tendency of such philosophers to take upon themselves the office of scrutinizing the springs of human action, with no other intent than to discover their imperfections. They employ their penetration, with invidious accuracy and malicious eagerness, to detect vices which were hidden from the world; they exhibit them with the ostentation of a discovery; they exaggerate them with every art and expedient their invention can suggest or their sagacity approve. This is the philosophical system of many a hermit. But be the success of such men's labours what it may, they will be so unfortunate as to find virtue enough in the world to defeat their hopes, and happiness sufficient to ensure their misery.

Upon the whole, perhaps, the philosophy of a recluse has little claim to our encouragement. That which is sometimes unfriendly, and generally useless, is seldom commendable. The knowledge which is cultivated, and not called into use for the public good, confers little benefit upon man; and the religion which is exercised in secret, with whatever fervour of devotion, loses much of its efficacy when it hides such an example from the world.

It is too often that these recluse and splenetic philosophers, whom I have mentioned, denounce their comprehensive anathemas against the sons of men, and condemn the whole species for the crime of an individual.

It is, perhaps, a dangerous indulgence, by which we ever allow ourselves to declaim in general terms against the depravity of human nature, and to give way to the too frequent tendency of our hearts, when we are irritated by particular offences, to say in our haste, 'All men are liars.'

It might not be amiss for those who are solicitous to supply their neighbours on every occasion with the apposite precepts of proverbial wisdom, to be cautious lest they become more desirous of indulging their spleen than their benevolence, more fond of correcting vice than reforming it, and lest they find more pleasure in the detection of evil than in the bringing good to light.   MONRO.

Nº 32. SATURDAY, OCTOBER 20, 1787.

The short and simple annals of the poor.—GRAY.

'TO THE AUTHOR OF THE OLLA PODRIDA.

'SIR,

'IF you should esteem this little tale worth a place in your amusing publication, you will probably hear more from him, who is yours,

A WANDERER.'

Being on a tour to the North, I was one evening arrested in my progress at the entrance of a small hamlet, by breaking the fore-wheel of my phaeton. This accident rendering it impracticable for me to proceed to the next town, from which I was now sixteen miles distant, I directed my steps to a small cottage, at the door of which, in a woodbine arbour, sat a man of about sixty, who was solacing himself with a pipe. In the front of his house was affixed a small board, which I conceived to contain an intimation, that travellers might there be accommodated. Addressing myself therefore to the old man, I requested his assistance, which he readily granted; but on my mentioning an intention of remaining at his house all night, he regretted that it was not in his power to receive me, and the more so, as there was no inn in the village. It was not till now that I discovered my error concerning the board over the door, which contained a notification, that there was taught that useful art, of which, if we credit Mrs. Baddeley's Memoirs, a certain noble lord was so grossly ignorant. In short, my friend proved to be the schoolmaster, and probably secretary to the hamlet. Affairs were in this situation when the vicar made his appearance. He was one of the most venerable figures I had ever seen; his time-silvered locks shaded his temple, whilst the lines of misfortune were, alas! but too visible in his countenance. Time had softened, but could not efface them. On seeing my broken equipage, he addressed me; and when he began to speak, his countenance was illumined by a smile.—'I presume, Sir,' said he, 'that the accident you have just experienced will render it impossible for you to proceed. Should that be the case, you will be much distressed for lodgings, the place affording no accommodations for travellers, as my parishioners are neither *willing* nor *able* to support an alehouse; and as we have few travellers, we have little need of one: but if you will accept the best accommodation my cottage affords, it is much at your service.' After expressing the sense I entertained of his goodness, I joyfully accepted so desirable an offer. As we entered the hamlet, the sun was gilding with his departing beams the village spire, whilst a gentle breeze refreshed the weary hinds, who, seated beneath the venerable oaks that overshadowed their cottages, were reposing themselves after the labours of the day, and listening attentively to the tale of an old soldier, who, like myself, had wandered thus far, and was now distressed for a lodging. He had been in several actions, in one of which he had lost a leg; and was now, like many other brave fellows,

—— Doom'd to beg
His bitter bread through realms his valour saved.

My kind host invited me to join the crowd, and listen to his tale. With this request I readily complied. No sooner did we make our appearance, than I attracted the attention of every one. The appearance of a stranger in a hamlet, two hundred miles from the capital, is generally productive of surprise; and every one examines the new comer with the most attentive observation. So wholly did my arrival engross the villagers, that the veteran was obliged to defer the continuation of his narrative till their curiosity should be gratified. Every one there took an opportunity of testifying the good will they bore my venerable host, by offering him a seat on the grass. The good man and myself were soon seated, and the brave veteran resumed his narrative in the following words:—' After,' continued he, ' I had been intoxicated, I was carried before a justice, who was intimate with the captain, at whose request he attested

me before I had sufficiently recovered my senses to
see the danger I was encountering. In the morning, when I came to myself, I found I was in custody
of three or four soldiers, who, after telling me what
had happened, in spite of all I could say, carried me
to the next town, without permitting me to take leave
of one of my neighbours. When they reached the
town it was market-day, and I saw several of the
people from our village, who were all sorry to hear
what had happened, and endeavoured to procure my
release, but in vain. After taking an affecting leave
of my neighbours, I was marched to Portsmouth, and
there, together with a hundred more, embarked for
the coast of Africa. During the voyage, most of our
number died, or became so enfeebled by sickness as
to make them unfit for service. This was owing
partly to the climate, partly to the want of water,
and to confinement in the ship. When we reached
the coast of Africa, we were landed, and experienced
every possible cruelty from our officers. At length,
however, a man of war arrived, who had lost several
mariners in a late action; and I, with some others,
was sent on board to serve in that station. Soon
after we put to sea, we fell in with a French man of
war. In the action I lost my leg, and was near
being thrown overboard; but the humanity of the
chaplain preserved my life, and, on my return to
England, procured my discharge. I applied for the
Chelsea bounty; but it was refused me, because I
lost my limb when acting as a marine : and, as I
was not a regular marine, I was not entitled to any
protection from the Admiralty ; therefore I am reduced to live on the good will of those who pity my
misfortunes. To be sure, mine is a hard lot; but
the king does not know it, or (God bless his majesty!)
he is too good to let those starve who have fought
his battles.

The village clock now striking eight, the worthy vicar rose, and, slipping something into the old man's hand, desired me to follow him. At our departure, the villagers promised to take care of the old man. We returned the farewell civilities of the rustics, and directed our steps to the vicarage. It was small, with a thatched roof. The front was entirely covered with woodbine and honeysuckle, which strongly scented the circumambient air. A grove of ancient oaks, that surrounded the house, cast a solemn shade over, and preserved the verdure of the adjacent lawn, through the midst of which ran a small brook, that gently murmured as it flowed. This, together with the bleating of the sheep, the lowing of the herds, the village murmurs, and the distant barkings of the trusty curs, who were now entering on their office as guardians of the hamlet, formed a concert, at least equal to that in Tottenham-court-road. On entering the wicket, we were met by a little girl of six years old. Her dress was simple, but elegant; and her appearance such as spoke her destined for a higher sphere. As soon as she had informed her grandfather that supper was ready, she dropped a courtesy, and retired. I delayed not a moment to congratulate the good old man on possessing so great a treasure. He replied, but with a sigh; and we entered the house, where every thing was distinguished by an air of elegant simplicity that surprised me. On our entrance, he introduced me to his wife; a woman turned of forty, who still possessed great remains of beauty, and had much the appearance of a woman of fashion. She received me with easy politeness, and regretted that she had it not in her power to entertain me better. I requested her not to distress me with unnecessary apologies, and we sat down to supper. The little angel, who welcomed us at the door, now seating herself opposite to me, offered me an opportunity of contemplating one of the finest faces I had ever beheld. My worthy host, observing how much I was struck with her appearance, directed my attention to a picture which hung over the mantel. It was a striking likeness of my little neighbour, only on a larger scale. 'That, Sir,' said he, 'is Harriet's mother. Do you not think here is a vast resemblance?' To this I assented; when the old man put up a prayer to Heaven, that she might resemble her mother in every thing but her unhappy fate. He then started another topic of conversation, without gratifying the curiosity he had excited concerning the fate of Harriet's mother, for whom I already felt myself much interested. Her tale, however, shall be the subject of a future paper.

X.   BERKELEY.

Nº 33. SATURDAY, OCTOBER 27, 1787.

'TO THE AUTHOR OF THE OLLA PODRIDA.

'SIR,

'I HAVE often beheld with concern the shameful condition of many churches in England; and I may venture to say, that the ruinous state in which they are suffered to continue, is one cause of the want of real piety in those who attend them. They must have a large stock of religion in their hearts, who can preserve any spirit of devotion in some of these fabrics, where there is frequently nothing to be seen or heard, which can fix the attention, or raise the mind to heaven. The Romanists adorn their churches with every thing which can make them appear grand, solemn, and like what is called the House of God.

Their music and singing are fine; and all things in their services and ceremonies conspire to raise their devotion.

'I was led to this subject by a late excursion into the country, to a village not twenty-five miles from London. The houses were much scattered about, and appeared beggarly; but within sight of the church there stood a gentleman's seat, which was laid out with all the elegance that could be bestowed upon the house and grounds. The churchyard joined to the park. Having surveyed every thing there, it being Sunday, I went into the church; to which one miserable bell, much like a small porridge-pot, called half a' dozen people, which number comprehended the congregation. The churchyard itself was low and wet; a broken gate the entrance; a few small wooden tombs and an old yew-tree the only ornaments. The inside of the church answered the outside: the walls green with damp; a few broken benches; with pieces of mats, dirty and very ragged; the stairs to the pulpit half worn away; the communion-table stood upon three legs; the rails worm-eaten, and half gone. The minister of this noble edifice was answerable to it in dress and manners. Having entered the church, he made the best of his way to the chancel, where he changed his wig, put on a dirty, iron-moulded, ragged surplice, and, after a short angry dialogue with the clerk, entered his desk, and began immediately without looking into the book. He read as if he had ten other churches to serve that day, at as many miles distance from each other. The clerk sung a melancholy solo; neither tune nor words of which I ever heard before. Then followed a short, confused, hurried discourse: after this the small congregation departed; which had consisted of a gentleman and his family from the distance of about a mile and a half, and two old men, who constantly attended for sixpence apiece, given by that family. The door was then shut, till the next Sunday came round.

'These are literally and truly facts: and that many other country churches are no better, either within or without, nor better served or attended, every body who has gone through the smaller villages in England must know. In some of the most admired parts of our admired country, in the neighbourhood of the capital, in parishes frequented by people of fortune, and where perhaps three or four noble families attend divine service every Sunday in the summer season, the churches are suffered, year after year, to be in a condition, in which not one of those families would suffer the worst room in their house to continue for a week.

'This deplorable state of our churches shews, I think, the state of piety amongst us more than any single circumstance, and has an effect upon the minds of young persons which is very discouraging. A wretched, cold, damp building, far removed often from all habitable dwellings; within sight of which few people of consequence care to live; made the receptacle of the dead; visited by the living only once a week; and then endangering the health of those who visit it,—do we wonder that people are glad to be dismissed from such a place, where nothing but horror and melancholy strike their eyes and their thoughts? Nor can the finest discourse from the pulpit dispel the gloom; and the psalmsinging in most country churches is far from contributing towards this salutary end.

'Who can expect that the young and gay will prefer this scene to the pleasures of the world? It is not in general to be expected. Would but the rich and great in every village, who lavish sums of money on their own persons, furniture, houses,

grounds, &c. &c.—would they but bestow a little of
it towards making the House of God, if not equal
with their own habitations, at least decent and cheerful, and such as may be entered safely and without
fear; very great indeed would be the effect on multitudes! It is difficult to conceive how a small portion of a large income can be expended more to the
credit of the donor, or to the benefit of his neighbours.

'We naturally call to mind, upon this occasion,
the uneasiness felt and expressed by the royal pro-
phet, on considering the magnificence of his own
house, and the little or no care taken of the ark of
God. And if we reflect seriously on the necessity
of having places consecrated to sacred purposes, and
the importance of their being kept up with due reve-
rence, two other remarkable passages in Holy Writ
will occur to every thinking person. When the second temple was built, and adorned by order of King
Artaxerxes, we find Ezra addressing himself to Heaven in these words: "Blessed be the Lord God of
our fathers, who has put such a thing as this into the
king's heart, to beautify the house of the Lord." And
we cannot but admire the wisdom of the Jews; who
when asking of our Lord a favour for the centurion,
say, "He loveth our nation, and hath built us a
synagogue." Then the Saviour went with them,

I am, Sir,

Your obedient humble servant,

A Friend to Decency in Religious Worship.'

The observations made by my correspondent are,
I fear, but too just; and I most readily embrace the
opportunity of recommending them to the consideration of all whom they may concern.

The inhabitants of most country parishes are prevented by their poverty from doing much in matters

of this kind. The necessary repairs are often a sufficient burden. Opulent families should therefore
step forward, and take upon them the articles of
ornament and beauty, or at least convenience and
comfort. They themselves would be the first to enjoy the advantages; of which it may not, surely, be
accounted the least, to be saved from the necessity
of blushing, when foreigners, or persons of a different
persuasion, behold the wretched condition of the
church by them frequented. A few good examples
could not fail of being followed; and fashion, in this
particular, might soon be put on the side of religion.

Indeed, unless the nobility and gentry shall be
pleased to lend their assistance, from having bad
churches we shall come to have none at all. Many
of them were built about the same time; and about
the same time, if not well looked to, will be falling:
and it is easier to support than to build.

It may be questioned, whether the Gothic form,
though so venerable for its antiquity, do not itself
occasion some of the inconveniences above lamented. A smaller and more compact room would often
contain the congregation; and the service might be
performed in it with more ease and benefit both to
the speaker and the hearer. It would be less subject
to damp and cold, and at the same time more light
and cheerful. For notwithstanding the celebrated
line of Milton, there is no natural connexion between darkness and religion, which is the source
of joy and comfort, of light and life, to the human
heart, and should dispel gloom and melancholy
wherever it comes.

Towards the promotion of this desirable end, a
due performance of psalmody could not fail greatly
to contribute, as it was most undoubtedly intended
to do. At present, in many country churches, it is
either dismal or ridiculous; and our people are fre-

quently induced to fall off to other religious assemblies, by the superior melody to be heard in them. There is hope, however, of some reformation among us in this part of divine worship; as many worthy clergymen have turned their thoughts this way, and selected proper tunes and proper words for the purpose. But whoever wishes to see this matter thoroughly discussed, and a proper plan proposed, must consult the sensible and excellent pamphlet lately published by Dr. Vincent on the subject.—Z.

BISHOP HORNE.

Nº 34. SATURDAY, NOVEMBER 3, 1787.

Fungar vice cotis.—Hor.

' TO THE AUTHOR OF THE OLLA PODRIDA.

' SIR,

' WHEN you commenced your career as a periodical editor, you enumerated, with a minuteness of detail, the various ingredients of which your farrago was to be composed. Having ever esteemed a discussion of the merits of literary compositions a very pleasing and profitable exercise of the judgment, with great satisfaction I perceived that criticism formed no inconsiderable part of your design. In your earlier numbers, my wishes were gratified by several judicious strictures on particular works of some ancient and modern writers. But lately, whether deeming such speculations unworthy of your attention, or catching the momentary but virtuous frenzy of reformation, you have devoted your lucubrations to objects, to which his majesty's most gracious proclamation, and the exertions of those intelligent magistrates, the justices, might be directed, with equal propriety, and perhaps with as great a probability of success.

'I mean not to reprehend your co-operative industry, but am desirous only of recalling to the recollection of your readers, that criticism was included in your original plan; and that the subject of this letter, though of a different complexion from some of your recent numbers, is not contradictory to the general tenor of your design.

'It is not my intention to trouble either you or your readers with remarks on any voluminous composition of eminent writers, or scrupulously to balance the nice discriminations of varying commentators. No, Sir, mine is a virgin theme, as yet untouched by the rude hand of criticism; and unrestrained by the galling shackles of prescriptive method; and, perhaps, my efforts may not be unattended with some advantage immediately to yourself, as the compositions to which I allude have commonly been diffused through periodical channels. These compositions are those narrations of blended fiction and sentiment, which, too inconsiderable from their size to swell into circulatory duodecimos, assume the general humble denomination of Tales, and are distinguished by the epithets *tender*, *pathetic*, *sentimental*, *founded on fact*, &c. &c.

'As Aristotle deduced his rules from the great originals who preceded him, it shall be my province to follow so illustrious an example, and in this primary essay to inculcate some general precepts, and not to point out in detail, or extract individual excellences which are profusely scattered through the ample labours of writers of this description.

'It is essential to a tale that it should be tender; for who is there that would not desire for his works the precious balm of a sigh or a tear, rather than that they should excite the applause of a smile or the boisterous acclamation of laughter?

' It should not abound too much in incident, lest the curiosity be excited as much as the finer feelings.

' The opening of a tale should be abrupt, and the author should commonly profess that his knowledge of it had arisen from some unforeseen accident. This saves the trouble of a long introduction, and brings the author and reader fairly at once into the subject. A piece of butter on a torn leaf, the being benighted on a long journey, the traveller's horse losing a shoe, have been such hackneyed expedients that I cannot possiby approve their repetition. The introduction of the mail-coach is however a new and fortunate epoch; and I doubt not of its being speedily adopted by several writers in every variation of fracture, until the whole stock of casualties be exhausted.

' The principal incident should not be extravagant, but be some common occurrence, that it may come home to the bosoms of a great number. A tender fair one seduced by her lover—a dutiful son turned out of doors by an unnatural father—a marriage of love and inclination thwarted by unfeeling parents—and all common events of a similar nature, are admirable topics.

' So much for the plot or ground-work, in which at intervals should be interspersed inferior circumstances, pathetic if possible; but the more minute they are, the greater will be their effect. A dog—a cow lowing for its calf—a weeping willow—a withered oak—an old woman—thin gray hairs on a human head—and the like, may certainly be introduced with great success.

' The diction may be allowed to be generally unequal, but should unquestionably be florid and elevated at those intervals of the narration where such embellishments may be requisite. Horace's prohibition of the " *purpurei panni* " must be totally disregarded.

'Exclamations should never be used without the most absolute necessity. They are a species of affront on the feelings of a reader, who throws down the book with indignation when he is informed at what passages he is to be affected. *Alas!* has had its day, and must now submit in its turn to the common chance of worldly revolutions. Indeed, it would be scarcely noticed, were not the mark of interjection *!* commonly annexed to it.—Dashes are more striking and pathetic—and are besides a very neat addition of typographical ornament.

'In respect to epithets, great caution is indispensable. The sun is ever *golden,* the moon ever *silver :* the sea is *azure,* and the meadow *verdant :* the foliage of the trees is commonly *green,* except in the sombre or dark-pathetic, when the autumnal tinge greatly enhances the pathos.

'Mythology and allegory must be introduced with circumspection. The *darts* of *Cupid,* the *fires* of *ambition,* the *warmth* of *love,* the *coldness* of *disdain,* from their general acceptation, may be used without danger.

'Allusions derived from natural philosophy are more novel and brilliant—*the electrical shock* of *passion,* the *vibration* of *reciprocal feelings,* and all phrases of the same cast, if the reader be a young lady at a boarding-school, or a young gentleman behind a counter, tend at once to dazzle and surprise.

'To insinuate or even to directly advance a coincidence between the hero or heroine, and any relative accompanying circumstance, is wonderfully efficacious, but is a felicity, though frequently attempted, not always attained by the most eminent authors. The following instances may probably exemplify my meaning: " In one corner of the field was a venerable elm, bare at the bottom, with its top scantily crowned with leaves, which formed no inapposite similitude of the venerable owner, verging to the grave by a gradual and natural decay :" this is of the latter kind. In the direct species may be classed such passages, as, " the lovely Maria, cherished by the tender care of a parent, delighted to contemplate the fragile and fragrant woodbine twining its slender folds around the supporting poplar."

‘ Though at first sight it may appear inconsiderable, it is really material to assign appropriate and characteristic names and places ; *Cassander, Cleora,* and all the list of romantic or historic appellations, have been long exploded, and invention is now freely permitted to create and to apply. The name of the hero should therefore excite respect by a due arrangement of harmonious and sonorous letters ; and that of the heroine should melt into liquid softness. Titles of amiable personages should gently flow ; such as are intended to create disgust, should hoarsely rumble.

‘ Place is far from being an unimportant consideration in the texture of tales. To introduce the reader to an amiable pair, sitting by a good coal-fire, is a minute but unsentimental circumstance. I would always therefore recommend a bower, which, though not common in real, is very convenient in fictitious gardens—but lest it might be mistaken for one of the lath edifices so frequent under this denomination in the vicinity of London, it should likewise be covered with honeysuckle or jasmine, " whose truant sprigs the heroine's gentle hand may be supposed to have conducted along the convex trellis."

‘ The *denouement* of a tale must be simple if the

principal incident be so. Yet it will admit endless variations, and in all cases, where the author is in the least degree embarrassed, a fragment is a never-failing expedient; and here I cannot but commend the great convenience of those intervals which occur in periodical publications; for by them an author is enabled to drop his narrative all at once, and to leave his reader for a week in an agreeable state of suspense and expectation.

'Morality, though not essential, is a pretty ornament to a tale; yet it should be sparingly adopted, I have ever greatly admired the insinuation which authors of this description so delicately convey respecting the conjugal fidelity of their married heroines; for we are universally informed, that the boys are the very pictures of their fathers, and that the girls have all the graces of their mothers.

'Such, Sir, are some of the opinions I have formed on this subject, which I have thrown together without order or connexion; and if from them the rising generation of tale-writers may cull any useful or improving hints, my ambition will be gratified. If *you* imagine that they may contribute to the amusement of the public, they are very much at your service.　　　　　　　　　　　　A. M.'

　　HAMMOND.

Nº 35.　SATURDAY, NOVEMBER 10, 1787.

Ille ego qui quondam——

'SIR,

'A CORRESPONDENT, who may or may not have engaged the attention of your readers, once more addresses you. My last letter to you, which contained an account of Mr. Hatchpenny, contained likewise my promise to give you some insight into the character of his wife. I shall therefore proceed in my plan without farther ceremony, notwithstanding that my correspondence with you has procured me, among my school-fellows, the title of *"The Sucking Socrates."*

'Mrs. Hatchpenny is that sort of woman, which the kindness or the sarcasm of the world (I am at a loss to say which) calls a managing housewife. Being rather limited in her ideas of human capacity, she considers it as the sum total of every virtue *to make things go as far as they can*, and the perfection of accomplishments to keep her house clean. Her refinements in economy are the general topics of her conversation, and she triumphs in defying her neighbours to say they ever saw a speck of dirt upon her hearth, or a chair out of its proper place.

'Not long ago I heard her informing a company, that she never hired a man-servant unless he could whistle. When her audience were staring at each other with looks of eager inquiry, she added, "when he goes to draw the beer, I constantly attend him to the top of the cellar-stairs, and insist upon his whistling all the time he remains below:" concluding naturally enough, that the same mouth cannot whistle and drink at the same time.

'My aunt makes her Solomon and me scrape our feet twenty times a day; and every Saturday night we are compelled to go up stairs without our shoes, because the house has been washed, and Molly has something else to do, besides *scrubbing after us for ever*.

'Notwithstanding her attention to economy, she is fond of fine clothes, or, as she calls it, *"looking like other people;"* to accomplish which, being now about eleven years past her meridian, and weighing about twenty-three stone avoirdupoise, she dresses herself in white, with a pink sash, and a proper assortment of pink ribands. If you have ever been so fortunate, gentle reader, as to catch an *Aurora borealis* in the *via lactea*, you cannot be at a loss for a simile to which you may liken the heroine of my history.

'The conversation of my aunt, particularly when she *looks like other people*, has something in it not perhaps very peculiar, yet not altogether unworthy of notice. She is what I have heard in the Borough called, *a fine spoken gentlewoman*; by which I am led to conceive their fine speaking consists in volubility of utterance, and a readiness in the vulgar tongue. Her speeches, however, are full of animated matter and rhetorical figure, and delivered in a tone of voice much like that of Caius Gracchus without his pitch-pipe. She talks of " *giving the hydra-head of fashion a rap on the knuckles;*" and, when she wants a simile, generally has recourse to a sugar-loaf, a roll of pig-tail, or the monument; sometimes however observing, that the coaches rattle by her door like *any thing*.

'Thus her style is ornamented with the best flowers of rhetoric, similes, and metaphors; similes which, by a peculiar felicity, convey no ideas of similitude; and metaphors which illustrate nothing but their own confusion.

'My aunt has many amiable qualities. Her fidelity to Solomon is unimpeached and invincible. She is constant in her attendance at church, unless perchance she has received a card of information, that Mrs. Deputy Peppercorn will wait on Mrs. Hatchpenny to dinner on Monday. In this case she prudently stays at home, whips up five syllabubs when there will be only four at dinner, returns her card of compliments, and waits with impatience to see Mrs. Peppercorn. The good lady has a just claim to the

title of compassionate. She cannot bear those vile
people who drive oxen through the streets of London, and *cut the poor creters about the legs till they
look enough to make one sick.* But compassion, which
consists only in words, does not content her. She
gives in charity to a poor boy every week a penny,
contriving within the seven days to send him at least
on fourteen errands. My aunt contents herself with
the idea that no one can say she is uncharitable. I
have somewhere heard of an ingenious philosopher,
who turned his shirt, and observed with the same
spirit of contentment and satisfaction, " *What a
comfort there is in clean linen!*"

'Mrs. Hatchpenny was so kind as to take me with
her, on Saturday last, to a tea-drinking party, at
Brompton, to which my uncle Solomon was invited;
but the wind being in the east, and stocks low, he
fancied he had a cold, and stayed at home. As we
went by appointment early, we had discussed some
weighty points before the tea entered. We had already learnt, that Miss Primrose gave fifteen shillings a yard for her apron, and that she bought it
from the shop at the corner of Juniper-street. Captain Makeweight had bruised his side by a fall in the
Artillery-ground, his sword getting between his legs,
and thereby laying him sprawling. Mr. Titus Oats,
a country cousin, had lost his turnips by the fly—
Miss Tallboy had sprained her ancle, by climbing
an apple-tree—Miss Posset had been at the Hack-
ney assembly ; and to be sure Miss Cardamum was
the belle of the place, till she began dancing, and
then she moved for all the world like a raw militia-
man to the quick march ; or, said the lady of the
house, with a good-humoured smile, " like an ele-
phant upon hot bricks"—" Or (added my aunt) like
St. Paul's upon four wheels." The tea now arrived ;
and between the rattling of the cups, we had only

time to fling in an observation or two like the chorus
of a Greek play, when the persons of the dialogue
are taking breath. We passed a few strictures upon
the widow Scramble's fourth marriage; and after
the removal of the tea-table, and a short review of
our absent neighbour's conduct, a general conversation took place, each addressing the person who sat
upon the nearest chair. My aunt, in the mean time,
could not help glancing first at the apron which had
created a former conversation, and then at her own,
being conscious that she had given two-and-twenty
shillings a yard for *every inch* of her's.—Unfortunately, no one asked the price of it, and she found
herself under the disagreeable necessity of informing the company, unsolicited, that she bought it
at the same time when Mr. Hatchpenny fined for
sheriff;—which is now seven years, come next Lord
Mayor. My aunt then took occasion to descant
upon the convenient situation of their shop in the
Borough; to do the business of which, she observed
with some emphasis, " they were obliged to keep
four journeymen, peck and perch all the year round,
one day with another."—Happily I was at hand to
explain to the company, which I did with great pleasure, that the words *peck* and *perch* (a favourite me-
taphor with my aunt) were an allusion to the inhabitant of a bird-cage, and meant nothing more than
board and lodging.

' " How do you like your neighbours the Hatchpennys?" said Miss Primrose, in a whisper to the
lady of the house.—" They are monstrously entertaining,"—said the other. A dialogue of a curious
nature then commenced, in which it was remarkable,
that the one regularly began a sentence, and the
other as regularly finished it. " As for him (said
the first) he's a churlish old fool, with all the qualities of a bear"—" except his dancing," returned the

other. "She's a great economist, I hear."—"Yes, in every thing but her speech."—"She's the envy of her neighbourhood, for her great prudence,"—"and her green pickles."—"Her reputation and her gown are ever without spot;"—"The one because she's so unreasonably ugly, and the other because she takes such excellent care of it."—"She's very nimble at cards"—"and, never having been detected in cheating, may be said to have had a perpetual run of good luck."—How far this dialogue proceeded, I know not, for our candle and lantern now called us to the peaceful abode of my uncle, whom, upon our return, we found, contrary to all the rules of domestic felicity, sitting with one foot upon the hearth, and a bottle by his side, which I strongly suspect to have contained some of the right Herefordshire. Upon our entrance, the position of the foot was quickly altered, and the bottle placed in the cupboard. My aunt withdrew, in order to divest herself of her splendour before the supper came; remarking, pointedly enough, that the *wear* and *tear* of clothes in carving was amazing and prodigious. The incidents of the next two hours were few, and may be easily told—Stocks had, from the accounts of that evening, risen one and a half, and my uncle's cold was better. At length, after a short dissertation upon the folly of mankind, and the extravagant demands of the Chelsea bun-makers, we recollected that it was Saturday night, pulled off our shoes, and retired to rest.   I am, &c.

MONRO.   SOCRATES IN EMBRYO.'

Nᵒ 36. SATURDAY, NOVEMBER 17, 1787.

Cum Græciam universam itinere rapido peragraverit, nihil fore de Græcià, nihil vere Atticum, aut quovis modo memorabile, domum reportabit; cum scilicet satis habuerit, peregrinantium plurimorum ritu, locorum nomina forsan et situs in transcursu notàsse; interea vero civium mores et instituta, præclara et virtutum et ingenii monimenta, oculo diligenti et curioso neutiquam exploraverit.—BURTONI *in* Πενταλογιαν *Dedicatio.*

THE various advantages which a traveller may derive from an acquaintance with the modern languages, are too obvious to require a minute detail. There is one, however, which deserves particularly to be pointed out; for, inconsiderable as it may appear in the estimation of young men of fortune, it will have no small weight with their parents and guardians. I allude to the considerable expense which may be prevented by those who are able to converse with the natives of other countries in their own language. He who is a tolerable linguist may be supposed to understand manners and customs ; and few men, however knavish, will attempt to cheat him who seems as wise as themselves. Ready and plausible conversation will disconcert the attacks of imposition, and elude the stratagems of chicane. The French imagine that England produces as much gold as the coast of Africa ; and that Monsieur John Bull leaves his native country merely to scatter his money with thoughtless profusion about the continent. In consequence of this extravagant opinion, he rarely escapes without paying five times the real value for every commodity. His pocket is supposed to be a rich bank, upon which every rapacious Frenchman may draw at pleasure ; and, of course, demands are made upon it with incessant avidity, and unrelenting ex-

tortion. These remarks are indebted for no small
degree of confirmation to the following authentic
anecdote. An officer of the regiment d'Artois, who
was on a journey from London to Paris, spent the
night at the *Hotel d' Angleterre*, at Calais. On examining his bill the next morning, he found that he
was charged a guinea for his supper, which had consisted only of cold meat and a bottle of *vin de pais*.
Enraged at so gross an imposition, he summoned the
master of the inn, and insisted upon an abatement.
'Milord,' said the landlord, 'I cannot disgrace
an Englishman of your rank by charging him a less
price.'—'Sirrah,' replied the officer, 'I am not a
man of quality, but a poor lieutenant in the service
of the Grand Monarque.'—'Morbleu!' rejoined
the landlord, 'I confess I have made an egregious
blunder.—I hope your honour will forgive me if I
reduce my demand to half-a-crown.'

It is not less necessary for a traveller to set out
with these qualifications, which will enable him to
repel the encroachments of imposition, than it is desirable for him to have stored his mind with domestic information. The author of the *Tableau de Paris*
remarks, with great justness, that we are not best
acquainted with those things which every day affords
us an opportunity of seeing. Curiosity is a languid
principle where access is easy, and gratification is
immediate : remoteness and difficulty are powerful
incentives to its vigorous and lasting operations. By
many who live within the sound of Bow bell, the internal wonders of St. Paul's or the Tower may not
be thought in the least degree interesting. Yet, how
justly would such persons be classed with the *incu-
rious* of Æsop, if, on visiting their country friends, it
should appear that they had never been in the whis-
pering gallery, or seen the lions ! Equally ridiculous
is that Englishman who roams in search of curiosi-

ties abroad, without having previously inspected the great beauties of nature and art at home. Sir Solomon Simple, before he was informed at Venice that the Pantheon, and St. Stephen's Walbrook, in London, were two of the first pieces of architecture in Europe, had never heard that such buildings existed.

When a man says he is going to visit foreign countries, it is necessary to be acquainted with his disposition and turn of mind, to understand what he designs by the declaration. The scholar, the connoisseur, the man of fashion, the merchant, intend to convey very different ideas by the same phrase. They may all be carried to the continent in the same ship, but, as their schemes are of the most dissimilar kinds, they separate never to meet again. Like the diverging rays of light, they all issue from the same point, but go off in various directions: their respective pursuits establish the analogy which is observed between travelling and the study of history. Characters, manners, customs, laws, government, antiquities, arts, sciences, and commerce, form the materials for observation to the traveller as well as the reader: these offer to both the highest, as well as the lowest, intellectual gratifications. The philosopher improves his theories by an intimate acquaintance with the characters of mankind; and the trifler kills his time in a manner entertaining to himself and inoffensive to the public.

It is the fashion of the present times to skim over the surface of things, and to dive to the bottom for nothing. General knowledge is most unquestionably most desirable, because it is best calculated for general intercourse with mankind. He, however, who dares to make false pretensions to it, meets with ridicule whilst he lays snares for applause. Such, likewise, is the reward of those who talk familiarly of persons whom they never knew, and describe places which they never saw. When fertility of invention deserts the standard of truth, to aid the boasts of vanity, it becomes not only a dangerous, but a despicable talent. Captain Lemuel Sinbad (who never extended his travels beyond Flanders) will tell you he shook hands with old Frederick the last time he reviewed his troops at Potsdam. Mention the Emperor of Germany, he will positively assert that he had a private conversation with him upon the improvement of gun-barrels. As for the earthquakes in Calabria, he accompanied Sir William Hamilton to ascertain the extent of their effects : he went frequently to shoot with the King of Naples ; and was informed at Constantinople, by a bashaw of three tails, that the Grand Seignior would certainly declare war against the Empress. The captain relates his incredible adventures in different companies with such material variations of circumstances, as repel belief, and destroy probability. He is generally as much at war with himself, as with the accounts given by others ; but neither the incredulous laugh, nor shrewd cavils of his friends, can cure him of his darling passion for fiction, because he can support the tottering fabric of romance with the props of subtle and prompt argument. Nothing pleases him more, than to find that the eel of sophistry will often elude the strongest grasp of objection. The captain bears a close resemblance to the noted Psalmanazar, to whom, when it was objected, that, as the sun was vertical at Formosa, all the fires must be extinguished, readily replied, ' that to prevent such inconveniences, the chimneys were built obliquely.'

By way of conclusion to this paper, such a sketch of character and detail of circumstances shall be exhibited as may probably be thought *Utopian*. Whether they be matters of fact or not, is by no means a subject of importance. If the plan laid down be practicable, the salutary effects resulting from its execution cannot be denied; because it will remove various inconveniences, and supply obvious defects in the instructions which have been frequently given to young travellers.

Frederick Manly, after having passed through a public school with applause, was sent to the university at the age of eighteen, under the immediate care of a private tutor. He applied with great diligence to classical and mathematical studies until he reached his twentieth year, when his father thought it was necessary for him to lay a solid foundation of domestic knowledge, before the superstructure of foreign travel was erected. This domestic knowledge consisted in an investigation of the principles of the constitution, the system of laws, and the administration of justice: it comprised a general inquiry into the several branches of commerce and manufactures; the state of agriculture, learning, and the arts; and concluded with an examination of the reasonableness of national religion. The defects or errors of books on these interesting topics, were remedied by conversations with intelligent persons; and the vague systems of theory were rectified by observations on the actual state of things. To diversify these pursuits, Manly made the regular tour of Great Britain, with the double intention of surveying natural and artificial curiosities, and of conversing with those who were eminent for manners, attainments, or genius. On visiting the continent, a more extensive and interesting prospect was displayed to his view; but he did not dissipate his curiosity amidst a frivolous and perplexing variety of objects. As he had been long habituated to the acquirement of useful knowledge, his researches were directed to that alone. He possessed the best means of procuring satisfactory and genuine information, as he conversed in the French, Italian, and German languages, with elegance and fluency. Such was the success with which he sacrificed to the Graces, that the ladies were charmed with the politeness of his manners; and such was the highly cultivated state of his mind, that foreigners, in general, gained considerably by the interchange of ideas. His heart was happily secured against the seductions of illicit amours, by an early attachment to a lady, whose temper and turn of mind were congenial with his own. Their absence was alleviated by a regular correspondence. His desire to contribute to her entertainment and information made every object doubly interesting, and gave the keenest edge to his curiosity. He surveyed the best specimens of ancient and modern art with a degree of rapture which bordered on enthusiasm. His taste was not the offspring of affectation, but the gift of nature, improved by experience. Harmony of colours, symmetry of parts, and the name of a great master, were, in his estimation, merely excellences of the second class. Sculpture and painting had no charms for him, exclusive of the force and beauty of their effect. Rome and Florence were the principal places of his residence, because in them the fine arts had deposited their most valuable treasures. At the expiration of three years he returned to his native country, and was united to the mistress of his affections. His manners were refined, but not formal; his dress was fashionable, but not foppish; his deportment easy, but not finical. His constitution was invigorated by exercise, and his fortune unimpaired by extravagance. Scepticism had not undermined, nor bigotry contracted, his religious principles. He gave a proof how high a polish the British diamond will take; his example fully evinced, that it cannot be excelled either in solidity or lustre. His prejudices were worn away by enlarged intercourse with mankind. His philanthropy was ardent, and his patriotism not less spirited than rational. Manly, in short, was a citizen of the world, who had carefully weighed the merits of all cultivated nations, and made England the place of his residence, because her excellences preponderated in the scale.   MONRO.

Nº 37. SATURDAY, NOVEMBER 24, 1787.

Continuation of the Vicar's Tale.

SUPPER being removed, after chatting some time, my worthy host conducted me to my bedchamber, which was on the ground floor, and lined with jasmine, that was conducted in at the windows. After wishing me good night, he retired, leaving me to rest. The beauty of the scenery, however, and my usual propensity to walk by moonlight, induced me to leave my fragrant cell. When I sallied forth, the moon was darting her temperated rays through the shade that surrounded the cottage, tipping the tops of the venerable oaks with silver. After taking a turn or two on the lawn, I wandered to the spot,— ' where the rude forefathers of the hamlet sleep.' It was small, and for the most part surrounded with yew-trees of an ancient date, beneath whose solemn shade many generations had mouldered into dust. No sooner did I enter, than my attention was caught by a pillar of white marble, placed on the summit of a small eminence, the base of which was surrounded with honeysuckles and woodbines, whilst a large willow overshadowed the pillar. As I was with attention perusing the epitaph, I was not a little alarmed by the approach of a figure, clothed in a long robe. The apparition continued advancing towards me with a slow step, and its eyes fixed on the ground, which prevented it observing me till we were within reach of each other. Great was my wonder at recognising my worthy host in this situation; nor was his astonishment less at finding his guest thus courting the appearance of goblins and fairies. After each had expressed the surprise he felt, I proceeded to inquire whose dust was there enshrined. To my question he returned answer, 'There, Sir, sleeps Harriet's mother, an innocent, but unfortunate woman. Pardon me, Sir,' said he, 'if for a moment I indulge my sorrow, and bedew my Harriet's grave with tears,—a tribute that I often pay her much-loved memory, when the rest of the world are lost in sleep.' Here he paused, and seemed much agitated. At length he requested me permission to defer the recital of Harriet's woes till the next day, as he found himself unequal to the task of proceeding in the painful detail. To this proposal I readily acceded, and we returned home. I retired to my room, but every attempt to procure sleep proved ineffectual: Harriet had so wholly occupied my thoughts, that no moment of the night was suffered to pass unnoticed. At length, 'when soared the warbling lark on high,' I left my couch, and rejoined my worthy landlord, who was busily employed in the arrangement of his garden. Though I declined mentioning the subject of our last night's adventure, yet he saw the marks of anxious expectation in my countenance, and proceeded to gratify the curiosity he had inspired. 'It will be necessary,' said he, ' before I proceed to relate the woes that befel my daughter, to give a short sketch of my own life. Six-and-twenty years ago, Mrs.*** came hither for the benefit of her health, the air being recommended as highly salubrious. On her arrival, she gave out that she was the daughter of a clergyman, who was lately dead, and had left her in narrow circumstances. I thought it my duty to visit her, and offer her any little attention in my power. She received me with politeness, and expressed a wish to cultivate my acquaintance. I continued to repeat my visits for some time, without suspecting that there was any thing particular in her history; till one morning, I found her in tears, reading a letter she had just received. On my entrance, she gave it to me: it contained a notification from Lord B.'s agent, that her usual remittances would no longer be continued. On opening this letter, I was led to suppose that her connexion with Lord B. was not of the most honourable nature: but all my suspicion vanished on her producing several letters from Lord B. to her mother, with whom he had been long connected. From these letters I learnt, that Mrs. *** was the daughter of Lord B. by Miss M. sister to a Scotch baronet, whom he had seduced and supported during the remainder of her life. But he had, it seems, determined to withdraw his protection from the fruit of their connexion. Mrs. *** declared she knew not what step to take, as her finances were nearly exhausted. I endeavoured to comfort her, assuring her that she should command every assistance in my power. On hearing this, she seemed a little satisfied, and became more composed. After sitting with her some time, I returned home, to consider in what manner I might most easily afford protection to the young orphan, whose whole dependance was on my support. If I took her home to live with me, as I was unmarried, it would give offence to my parishioners: my income was too confined to admit of my affording her a separate establishment. Thus circumstanced, I determined to offer her my hand. You will, no doubt, say it was rather an imprudent step for a man who had seen his fortieth year to connect himself with youth and beauty; but as my brother was then living, it was impossible for me to render her the least assistance on any other plan. She received my proposal with grateful surprise, and accepted it without hesitation. In a few days we were married, and have now lived together six-and-twenty years, in a state, the felicity of which has never been interrupted by those discordant jars which are so frequently the concomitants of matrimony: though, alas! our peace has received a mortal wound from one, the bare mention of whose name fills me with horror! But not to digress—before the return of that day which saw me blessed with the hand of Emily, my happiness received an important addition, by the birth of a daughter, who inherited all her mother's charms. It is superfluous to add, that she was equally the idol of both her parents; and as she was the only fruit of our marriage, she became every day a greater favourite. My wife had received such an education as rendered her fully capable of accomplishing her daughter in a manner far superior to any thing her situation required, or, perhaps, could justify. To this agreeable employment, however, she devoted her whole time; and when Harriet had reached her eighteenth year, she was, in every respect, a highly accomplished woman. She was become what that picture represents her. With an amiable temper and gentle manners, she was the idol of the village. Hitherto she had experienced a state of felicity unknown in the more exalted stations of life—unconscious, alas! of the ills that awaited her future years.

It is with reluctance I proceed in the melancholy narrative. One evening, as a young man, attended by a servant, was passing through the village, his horse startled, and threw him. Happening to be on the spot at the time, I offered every assistance in my power, and conveying him to my cottage, dispatched his servant in quest of a surgeon, who declared our patient was not in any danger, but recommended it to him to delay his departure for a day or two. His health however, or rather his love, did not admit of his travelling for near a fortnight; during which time, he established his interest with Harriet by the most pleasing and unremitting attention to her slightest wishes. When about to depart, he requested leave to repeat his visit on his return from his intended tour, dropping, at the same time, some distant hints of his affection for Harriet, to whom he was by no means indifferent.

'Mr. H. (for so our guest was named) informed us, previous to his departure, that he had a small independent fortune; but that from a distant relation he had considerable expectation. After bidding an affectionate adieu to Harriet, he set out on his intended tour, which lasted for a month.'—The effects produced by his absence must, however, be reserved for another paper.—X.   BERKELEY.

Nº 38. SATURDAY, DECEMBER 1, 1787.

Conclusion of the Vicar's Tale.

'DURING the time of Mr. H's absence, Harriet appeared pensive, and I observed with pain that he had made no slight impression on her heart. At length Mr. H. returned, and Harriet's reception of him left us no room to doubt her attachment. During his second visit he was very assiduous to secure the

favour of all the family : with Harriet he easily succeeded ; nor were Mrs. T. or myself disposed to dislike him. His manners were elegant, and his wit
lively. At length he obtained from Harriet the promise of her hand, provided her parents should not
object. Hitherto I had never been induced to make
any inquiries concerning his circumstances and character. Now, however, by his direction, I applied
to Mr. E—ns, a clergyman of his acquaintance.
This gentleman, now in an exalted station in the
church, then chaplain to Lord C. informed me, that
Mr. H. was in every respect a desirable match for
my daughter; and that, whenever his cousin should
die, he would be enabled to maintain her in affluence
and splendour :—he added that his character was
unexceptionable. Little suspecting the villanous
part Mr. E—ns was acting, I readily consented to
the proposed union, and performed the ceremony
myself. Mr. H. requested that their marriage might
be kept a secret till the birth of a son and heir.
This proposal rather alarmed me but it was too late
to retreat ; and knowing no one in the great world,
it was impossible for me previous to the marriage,
to procure any account of Mr. H. but such as his
friend communicated to me. Thus circumstanced,
I could only consent : and as Harriet readily adopted every proposal that came from one she so tenderly
loved, the matter was finally agreed on. After stay-
ing a few days, he set off for London, but soon returned, and passed the whole winter with us; and
in the spring Harriet was delivered of that little girl
you so much admire. I now pressed him to acknowledge my daughter as his wife. To this he answered, that, had she brought him a son, he would readily have complied with my request; but that his
cousin was so great an oddity, that he could not
bear the idea (to use his own expression) ' of hav-

ing his fortune lavished in a milliner's shop :—but,' added he, ' if you insist upon it, I will now risk the loss of all his fortune, and introduce my Harriet to his presence. Harriet, however, again interfered, and desired that Mr. H. might not be forced into measures that might in the end prove destructive of his future prospect, and induce him to regret the day he ever saw her. These arguments prevailed, and Mr. H. was suffered to continue as a member of the family without any farther notice being taken of the subject. In this manner had three years elapsed undistinguished by any remarkable event, Mr. H. generally passing half the year with us, and the remainder in London, attending, as he said, on his cousin ; when one day, as he was sitting with us at dinner, a chaise and four drove up to the house. The servants inquired for Mr. H. and on hearing he was there, opened the carriage door. A gentleman, dressed like an officer, jumped out, followed by a lady in a travelling dress ;—they rushed immediately into the room. Their appearance amazed us ; but Mr. H. betrayed the most visible marks of consternation. The lady appeared to be about thirty. She was a woman by no means destitute of personal charms. The moment she entered the room, she seized upon Harriet, and, loading her with every horrible epithet, proceeded to indulge her passion by striking her innocent rival. On seeing this, an old servant of mine seized the lady and forcibly turned her out of the house ; then fastened the door. It was not till now that we perceived the absence of Mr. H. who had, it seems, retired with the lady's companion. Whilst we were still lost in amazement at the transaction we had just witnessed, we were alarmed to the highest pitch by the report of a pistol. Harriet instantly fainted. Whilst Mrs. T. was recovering her, I flew to the spot from whence the sound proceeded, and there found Mr. H. weltering in his blood, with a pistol lying by him. I approached, and found him still sensible. He informed me, that the lady's brother and he had fought, and that seeing him fall, they had both escaped as fast as possible. I instantly procured assistance, and conveyed him to the house, where he was put to bed, and a surgeon was sent for. In the mean time Harriet had several fits, and we were very apprehensive that the hour of her fate was approaching. On the arrival of the surgeon, he declared the wound Mr. H. had received would probably prove mortal, and recommended the arrangement of his affairs. Mr. H. received the news with great agony, and desired that I might be left alone with him. No sooner was this request granted, than he addressed me in the following terms: ' In me, Sir, behold the most unfortunate, and, alas! the most guilty of men. The lady, whose ill-timed visit has lost me my life, is,—I tremble to pronounce the word,—my wife.' Seeing me pale with horror, he proceeded: ' No wonder, Sir, that you should behold with horror one who has repaid *unbounded hospitality* by *unequalled villany*. The bare remembrance of my own guilt distracts me. The awful hour is now fast approaching, when I must receive my final doom from that Heaven whose laws I have so daringly violated. To redress the injuries I have committed is, alas! impossible. My death will be an atonement by no means sufficient. I cannot, however, leave this world till you shall be informed, that ten thousand pounds, the whole of my property that is at my disposal, has long ago been transferred by me into the hands of trustees, for the benefit of my much-injured Harriet, and her unhappy infant. In my own defence I have nothing to urge. Suffer me only to remark, that my misfortune arose from the avarice of my father, who

forced me into a marriage with the woman you lately
saw, and whose brother has been the instrument in
the hand of Providence to inflict on me the doom I
so much merited. If possible, conceal from Harriet
that I was married. Picture, for her sake, an innocent deception, and tell her that I was only engaged
to that lady. This will contribute to promote her
repose, and the deception may possibly plead the
merit of prolonging a life so dear to you : for the
elevated mind of my Harriet would never survive the
fatal discovery of my villany. But, oh! when my
unhappy child shall ask the fate of him who gave
her being, in pity draw a veil over that guilt which
can scarcely hope to obtain the pardon of Heaven.'
There he ceased, and, uttering a short prayer, expired. Happily for Harriet, she continued in a state
of insensibility for three days, during which time I
had the body removed to a neighbouring house,
there to wait for interment. Having addressed a
letter to Mr. H.'s agent in town, he sent orders for
the body to be removed to the family burying-place,
where it was accordingly interred. Harriet recovered by slow degrees from the state of happy insensibility into which the death of Mr. H. had plunged
her. Her grief became silent and settled. Groans
and exclamations now gave way to sighs and the
bitter tears of desponding grief. She seldom or
never spoke; but would cry for hours together over
her hapless infant, then call on the shadow, of her
departed Henry, little suspecting the irreparable injury he had done her. It was with infinite anxiety
I beheld the decline of Harriet's health. Prone as
we ever are to hope what we ardently desire, I now
despaired of her recovery. Whilst in a state of
hopeless inactivity, I was doomed to witness the
lingering death of my lamented Harriet, I received
a visit from an old friend. On his arrival, I allotted

him the apartment formerly inhabited by Mr. H. and
Harriet. About midnight he was awoke by some
one entering the apartment. On removing the curtain, he discovered, by the light of the moon, my
adored Harriet in a white dress. Her eyes were
open, but had a vacant look, that plainly proved she
was not awake. She advanced with a slow step;
then seating herself at the foot of the bed, remained
there an hour, weeping bitterly the whole time, but
without uttering a word. My friend fearful of the
consequences, forbore to awake her, and she retired
with the same deliberate step she had entered. This
intelligence alarmed me excessively. On the next
night she was watched and the same scene was repeated, with this difference, that, after quitting the
fatal apartment, she went to the room where her
daughter usually slept, and laying herself down on
the bed, wept over the child for some time; then returned to her apartment. The next morning we
waited with anxiety for her appearance at breakfast;
but, alas!—'—Here a flood of tears afforded to my
friend that relief which he so much needed; and we
returned to the house. After passing some days
with this worthy couple, I proceeded on my tour;
quitting, with reluctance, the abode of sorrow and
resignation.—Those whom the perusal of this tale
may interest, will, if ever they visit the banks of the
Alma, find that the author has copied his characters
from nature.—X.   BERKELEY.

N° 39. SATURDAY, DECEMBER 8, 1787.

Τιμβωτε στηλητε·το γαρ γερας εστι θανοντων.—Iliad, xvi. 457.

What honours mortals after death receive,
Those unavailing honours we may give.—POPE.

THAT fame is the universal passion is by nothing more conspicuously discovered than by epitaphs. The generality of mankind are not content to sink ingloriously into the grave, but wish to be paid that tribute of panegyric after their deaths, which in many cases may not be due to the virtues of their lives. If the vanity of the departed has not been provident of monumental honours, the partiality of friends is eager to supply them. Death may be said with almost equal propriety to confer as well as to level all distinctions. In consequence of that event, a kind of chemical operation takes place; for those characters which were mixed with the gross particles of vice, by being thrown into the alembic of flattery, are sublimated into the essence of virtue. He who, during the performance of his part upon the stage of the world, was little if at all applauded, after the close of the drama, is pourtrayed as the favourite of 'every virtue under heaven.' To save the opulent from oblivion, the sculptor unites his labours with the scholar or the poet, whilst the rustic is indebted for his mite of posthumous renown to the carpenter, the painter, or the mason. The structures of fame are in both cases built with materials whose duration is short. It may check the sallies of pride to reflect on the mortality of man; but for its complete humiliation let it be remembered, that epitaphs and monuments decay. Had not Cicero been assisted by his memory, he could never have deciphered the mutilated verses on the tomb of Archimedes. The antiquarian searches in vain for the original inscriptions on Chaucer and Sidney.

The observations of the illustrious Johnson on epitaphs are marked with acuteness as well as extent of judgment. In his criticisms, however, on those of Pope, he has shewn a petulance of temper and fastidiousness of taste, at the same time that he acknowledged the barrenness of Pope's topics, and the difficulty of distributing to numbers that praise which is particular and characteristic. He who is a critic should consider, that, according to the natural progress of human opinions, he may become the subject of criticism. If Johnson had ever conjectured that he must one day be tried by his own laws, more lenity would probably have been shewn to Pope. The doctor remarks, ' that an epitaph ought not to be longer than common beholders have leisure and patience to peruse.' Of the few he has left behind him, that on Hanmer is surely objectionable for its prolixity. He reprobates with just severity any allusions to classical customs, and the situation of Roman tombs. The lines of Passeratius on Henry of France are quoted, to shew the impropriety of addressing the reader as a traveller. Yet the doctor forgot his strictures and his quotation when he concluded his character of Thrale with *Abi, viator.*

The preceding remarks are intended as an introduction to a plan which I take this opportunity of laying before the public. It is my design to publish a collection of the most remarkable epitaphs, with critical observations. Particular attention will be paid to their arrangement, of which it shall be the object of the remaining part of this paper to exhibit an exact specimen. Without spinning too many threads of classification, a few striking and general distinctions only shall be adopted: the *Learned*—the *Sublime*—the *Characteristic*—the *Complimentary*. The first class is intended to allure the scholars of our famous universities to subscribe liberally to the work.   To let the reader into a secret, it was originally my design to have published this part in a folio by itself, with a pompous dedication.   Happening to see a goose singed with a leaf of the *Pietas Oxoniensis*, I was frightened from the prosecution of my plan by so unlucky an omen.   My intended work will, notwithstanding, comprise learning enough to satisfy the appetite of a reasonable linguist.   There will be no room for complaint if I begin with Persian, and end with Latin.   The first epitaph shall be that on Hadgi Shaughsware, in Saint Botolph's Bishopsgate; and the last shall be the laconic *Fui Caius*, at Cambridge.

Under this head, many ingenious and novel opinions will be advanced relative to the *language* as well as the *sentiments* of these compositions.   It will be proved to a demonstration, that the *learned* languages are absurdly used except for *learned* men. Some one has well observed, that, if the dead could hear their own sepulchral praise, they would be put to the blush.   Some, without doubt, would with amiable diffidence adopt the elegant sentiments of Frontinus, *Impensa monimenti supervacua est; memoria nostri durabit, si vitâ meruimus.*—'Superfluous is the expense of the tomb, since our memory will flourish if our conduct has merited that honour.'   But multitudes must be insensible to the emotions of shame, unless they were endued with the gift of tongues. The moral design of an epitaph is to inspire an emulation of the virtues of the deceased.   This cannot be effected, unless the language which records those virtues be intelligible to persons who are in a situation to emulate them.   The talents and munificence of Busby and South are transmitted to scholars by a vehicle which is familiar to them; but how can the ladies improve by the example of the beautiful Mrs. Arundel, who is celebrated in a Latin inscription in Saint Mary's Oxford? or how is the courage of our sailors likely to be increased by the Ciceronian periods on Rooke at Canterbury?

The *Sublime.*—This species is confined to those who occupy the most distinguished niches in the temple of Fame. Simplicity and brevity are its characteristics. Such names as Bacon, Locke, and Newton, want not the flowers of eloquence, or the parade of periods, to decorate their monuments. The tomb of Sir Christopher Wren has a local propriety from his being buried in Saint Paul's, which gave birth to an inscription worthy of that illustrious restorer of Attic architecture.

Subtus conditur hujus ecclesiæ et urbis conditor, qui vixit annos ultra nonaginta, non sibi sed bono publico. Lector, si monimentum requiris, circumspice.

The *Characteristic.*—A class which far excels all the rest, as it contains examples of splendid talents and eminent virtues marked with peculiar and appropriate praise. Not only those epitaphs wherein their due measure of applause is distributed with nice discrimination to philosophers, poets, warriors, and statesmen, will be introduced under this head, but such likewise as have preserved the memory of the lowly and the ignoble. These compositions are as difficult to be met with as accurate miniatures. Dr. Johnson would have said that Pope's verses on Mrs. Corbet was a very proper exemplification of this species. Perhaps the following by Hawkesworth, in Bromley churchyard, is by no means inferior to it:

'Near this place lies the body of Elizabeth Monk, aged 101, the wife of John Monk, blacksmith, by whom she had no children. But virtue would not suffer her to be childless. An infant, to whom, and to whose father and uncles she had been nurse, became dependant upon strangers for the necessaries of life: to him she afforded the protection of a mother. This parental charity was returned with filial affection, and she was supported in the feebleness of age by him whom she had cherished in the helplessness of infancy. Let it be remembered, that there is no station in which industry will not obtain power to be liberal, nor any character on which liberality will not confer honour. She had long been prepared, by a simple and unaffected piety, for her end. To preserve the memory of this person, but yet more to perpetuate the lesson of her life, this stone was erected by voluntary contribution.'

The *Complimentary.*—This article comprises inscriptions, in which the dead are more indebted for their praise to invention than to merit. The writers of epitaphs ought to be historians, and not poets.

Their panegyric often fatigues with prolixity, and disgusts with fulsomeness. Take away the dates from complimentary epitaphs, and they have all the appearance of dedications. They exhibit the demigods of the golden age, or the immaculate heroes of romance. Like Addison's Cato, they seem to have been out of the reach of human passions or infirmities—of a nature too much exalted to excite pity, and famed for excellences too transcendent for imitation. Sometimes, however, it happens, that common topics of encomium are touched with so masterly a hand, that they charm with an irresistible grace, and have all the force of novelty. For a panegyrist to declare, *that a lady is deserving of the highest praise—that she is as beautiful as an angel*—and *that she is remarkable for uniform piety*—seems as if he could not strike out of the beaten track. But surely it is out of the power of a vulgar bard to pourtray such ideas in the following manner:

On Lady Catherine Paston, Paston Church, Norfolk,
1628.

> Can man be silent, and not praises find
> For her who lived the praise of woman-kind?
> Whose outward frame was lent the world, to guess
> What shapes our souls shall wear in happiness.
> Whose virtue did all ill so overswaye,
> That her whole life was a communion-daye.

As my publication will be extended only to those epitaphs which are really inscribed on tomb-stones, the *ludicrous* and the *gay* will of course be omitted. Let him whose inclination may lead him to peruse such, be referred to magazines and jest-books. He will there find that Epigram, Pun, Satire, and Burlesque, have attempted to throw a gleam of levity upon a subject which is too awful to be made ridiculous. Wit and humour never more mistake their object, than when they aim their shafts at man in a state of dissolution. But, however wanton and injudicious their sallies have been, they have never profaned the sanctity of Christian temples by affixing their productions to them. Such an indecorum militates too strongly against piety and sensibility to be tolerated with patience. To sport with the characters of the departed is a sufficient triumph for gaiety, without being permitted to erect a trophy over their graves.

The perusal of epitaphs is not to be considered as a frivolous and light amusement. If such only be the objects of attention as have been noticed with our applause, it is unquestionably an introduction to pleasing knowledge, and an incentive to moral improvement. What biography is to history, an epitaph is to biography. It is a sketch which marks the great outlines of character, and excites curiosity to view the portraits as painted on the pages of history. It is likewise an epitome of a sermon, which teaches the most useful truths in the most concise form. Monumental inscriptions remind us, that time is on the wing,—that every rank and age must fall a prey to his depredations,—that the moments of life are too precious to be squandered away on trifles,—that religion is the only support against the fears and the pains of death, and the only guide to the joys of eternity.—Q.   KETT.

Nº 40. SATURDAY, DECEMBER 15, 1787.

Carpimus indecores joculari carmine mores.

For the substance of this paper, I have ventured to make an extract from a very pleasant and witty Latin author, who wrote about two hundred and thirty years ago. To which I have subjoined what may be more properly called a paraphrase than a translation.

The book I allude to is entitled, *De Morum Simplicitate, auctore Frederico Dedekindo*, a poem, in three books. The author was a German, and his work, I believe, gave rise to that species of humour, of which Swift shewed himself completely master, in his 'Advice to Servants,' and which has been since imitated in publications of very modern date;—particularly in 'Advice to Officers,' and the 'Facetious Hints of Geoffrey Gambado, Esq.' I know not that Swift has any where mentioned this author, though his works contain many passages which incline me to believe he had perused him with considerable attention. I have extracted the first chapter of his first book, in order to give some specimen of that style, whose origin has been attributed to various writers, in various times and countries, some giving it to Rabelais, and others to Cervantes. Dedekindus appears, from his preface and conclusion, to have been a man of great sense and refined manners. That he has fallen into obscurity, is, perhaps, to be attributed to the few copies of his works of which the world is in possession. His versification has the ease and elegance of Ovid. Every critic will discover that he has not the purity of the Augustan age; yet every one will read him with pleasure, who is not too fastidious to be easily pleased.

Since I read his book, and rendered the sentiments, as near as I could, of the first chapter, into English, I have discovered, that the work has been translated by a Mr. Bull, in 1739, and dedicated, very properly, to Dean Swift, who first (as the translator says) introduced into these kingdoms of Great Britain and Ireland an ironical manner of writing, to the discouragement of vice, ill-manners, and folly, and the promotion of virtue, good-manners, and good sense.

The original contains an apology at the beginning, and another at the end, for the indelicacy into which the author is unavoidably led. The *fidus interpres* lived at a time when such a kind of wit met with a patron in almost every reader. He seems rather to have laboured in expressing fully every gross idea which ought to have been softened, or might have been omitted without injuring the work.

The preface and conclusion are improperly passed over without any notice by the translator. Upon the whole, the fate of the translation (which is at present almost totally unknown) is not to be lamented. The author of the following version will

be amply rewarded for his pains, if he can be in the
smallest degree instrumental in bringing forward the
original into that notice which it manifestly merits.

Quæ modestia servanda sit mane in vestitu, capillis,
facie, et dentibus mundandis.

Quisquis habes odio rigidi præcepta magistri,
    Qui nisi de morum nil gravitate docet,
Huc propera, et placidis utentem vocibus audi :
    Non tonat hîc aliquis tristia verba Cato.
Da mihi te docilem crasso sermone loquentem ;
    Nec dubita, parvo tempore doctus eris.
Discipulus, facili superare labore magistrum,
    Crede mihi, antiquâ simplicitate, potes.
Et licet hæc aliquis rigidâ de gente sophorum
    Vituperet, morum quæ documenta damus ;
Non tamen illa tibi quidquam nocuisse videbis ;
    Sedula si Musæ jussa sequère meæ.

I.

Fulcra soporiferi eum liqueris alta cubilis,
    (Quod fieri medium non decet ante diem)
Egregie civilis eris, si nulla parentes
    Mane salutandi sit tibi cura tuos.
Non homini cuiquam felicia fata preceris,
    Sæpe tibi grates dicere ne sit opus.
Prospera quantumvis optes, quid proderit illis ?
    Optima non damnum est perdere verba leve.
Gens sine mane suos Hebræa salutet amico,
    Quam tenet implicitam multa superstitio.
Cur tibi tam levium sit cura superflua rerum ?
    Canitiem justos cura dat ante dies.

II.

Non habet exiguas quoque pandiculatio vires,
    Si medicos par est credere vera loqui.
Accidit ex longo nervos torpere sopore,
    Atque male officii munus obire sui.
Excitat hos certo tibi pandiculatio motu
    Utere : nec mores dedecet illa tuos.

III.

Nec reliquis surgens te vestibus indue, nudæ
    Indusium satis est imposuisse cuti.
Sed reliquas geminis vestes complectitor ulnis,
    Aspera si duro frigore sævit hiems.

Scilicet in calido jucundius est hypocausto
    Induere, a sævo ne violère gelu.
Nec moveat, virgo vel femina si sit ibidem :
    Tu tamen uteris moribus usque tuis.
Sique tuis quisquam factis offenditur, illum,
    Cernere si talem nolit, abire jube.
Quisque tibi cedat, nec tu concesseris ulli :
    Conditione tuâ es liber, et esse velis.

IV.

Tandem ubi vestitus fueris, pendere solutas
    In genibus caligas (res decet illa) sines.
Namque ita virginibus tacitâ ratione placebis,
    Teque sibi optabit quæque puella virum.
Non sat eris simplex, si corpus, vane, ligare
    Cœperis ; et ventri vincula dura nocent.

V.

Ne nimis evadas moratus, pectere crines
    Neglige ; neglecta est forma decora viro.
Femineæ crines ornare relinquito turbæ ;
    Comantur juvenes quos levis urit Amor.
Crede mihi, dominum te nulla puella vocabit,
    Si te composito viderit esse vilo.
' Sint procul a nobis juvenes ut femina comti ;'
    Scribit Amazonio Cressa puella viro.
Eximio tibi erit decori, si pluma capillis
    Mixta erit, et laudem providus inde feres.
Scilicet hoc homines poteris convincere signo,
    Non in stramineo te cubuisse toro.

VI.

Sint capitis crines longi, non forcipe tonsi,
    Cæsaries humeros tangat ut alta tuos,
Tutus ut a tristi rigidæ sis frigore brumæ,
    Vertice prolixus crinis alendus erit.
Cuncti homines quondam longos habuère capillos,
    Quas modo virgineus curat habere chorus.
Regna pater quando Saturnus prisca tenebat,
    Tunc fuit in longis gloria magna comis.
Simplicitas veterum laudatur ubique virorum :
    Quâ potes, hos semper sit tibi cura sequi.

VII.

Dedecus esse puta faciemve manusve lavare ;
    Commodius crasso sordet utrumque luto.
' Qui volet his vesci, per me licet ipse lavabit,'
    Dicito : ' res curæ non erit illa mihi.'

VIII.

Forsan erit dentes qui te mundare monebit,
    Sed monitis parens inveniêre cave.
Recta valetudo corrumpi dicitur oris,
    Sæpe novâ si quis proluat illud aquâ.
Quid noceat, dentes quod sint fuligine flavi?
    Iste color rubei cernitur esse croci.
Iste color fulvo quoque non culpatur in auro,
    Auro, quod nunquam non amat omnis homo.
Dentibus ergo tuis cur sit color ille pudendus?
    Si sapis, hanc a te fac procul ire fidem.

Forced to be grave, though wishing much to smile,
Who hears, impatient of the humdrum style,
Grave preachers, on grave subjects, gravely prose,
So dull they tempt, so loud they mock repose;
Let him to me, in gayer mood, attend,
Nor dread some thundering Cato in a friend.
If aught my song avail, 'tis plain, not nice,
He'll prove a finish'd scholar in a trice,
To vent their spleen, elate with learned pride,
My theme let schoolmen, if they will, deride:
With willing ear who listens to my rules,
Shall hear unmoved the clamours of the schools.

I.

Quit, quit thy bed, what time the busy sun
('Twere vulgar sooner) half his course hath run.
No kind return maternal care demands;
And scorn the blessing from a father's hands.
Let others hail the day with praise and prayer,
Eternal gratitude's eternal care.
For common welfare let the fond fool pray,
(With many a godly sentence thrown away)
To whom Religion in her zeal hath given
Dire superstition and a fear of Heaven.
Far, far from thee, be such ignoble aims:
Life with dull Care all fellowship disclaims.

II.

To stretch and yawn is great relief to some,
Bracing the slacken'd nerve with sleep o'ercome.
This Doctor Filgrane stoutly will maintain:
And shall apothecaries talk in vain?
Besides, how pleasing 'tis some youth to see,
Gape, stretch, and yawn, and all that, gracefully?

III.

Be sure, with half your clothes thrown on, to stand
(Coat, stockings, garters, dangling in your hand),
Close o'er the parlour fire; for thee 'twas made;
Nor let the cold thy gentle limbs invade.
O'er the same fire though nymph or matron glow.
'Twere but false modesty should bid you go.
If friends too nice your plan to censure move,
Bid them begone to scenes they more approve.
To thee, no doubt, all things, all men shall bend:
Thy right is liberty, thy right defend.

IV.

At length you're dress'd; take care, below the knees,
Let the loose boot hang down with graceful ease.
In this, some nameless grace, some charm unknown,
Wins the whole sex, and every girl's your own.
Loose let your waistcoat fly, while snug your chin
Lies couch'd behind a well-spread chitterlin.

V.

To tend with anxious touch the plaited hair,
Leave to the love-sick school-boy and his fair.
Do thou step forth in easy dishabille,
Your uncombed ringlets floating as they will;
For beaux so finical in dress and air
Scarce get a scrawl from Chloe once a year.
Thus to her lover writes the Cretan lass :
' I hate these coxcombs, that before their glass
For ever fix'd, are nothing till they're dress'd,
And then but bearded women at the best.'
All from the downy bed you'll haply bear,
('Tis no small grace) a feather in your hair;
From which mankind this inference may draw :
' Ne'er sleeps the gentle youth on bed of straw.'
A praise so easily, so nobly won,
What beau, what prudent beau, would ever shun!

VI.

To crop thy flowing hair, lo ! ready stands
The ruthless barber with unhallow'd hands.
Fly, fly his touch; you'll wish, amid the snow,
Beneath your wonted periwig to glow.
In times of old, by ribbon unconfined,
Their long lank locks were glory of mankind.

Such locks the nymphs now wear in silks who rustle,
In rich luxuriance reaching to the bustle.
Fie on our bob-tail'd race, these days are o'er,
And Time shall see straight heads of hair no more!

VII.

Some souse in water every morn their face,
And think clean hands give something of a grace.
Who on their fingers feed for lack of meat,
Such men should wash their food before they eat.

VIII.

Some are such fools, they clean their teeth, and cry,
An unclean tooth is loathsome to the eye.
Take heed, dame Nature says; obey her laws;
Cold water is the devil in your jaws.
What though your grinders, odious to the view,
Vie with the crocus in her yellow hue,
Or golden guinea to exceed aspire?
The crocus and the guinea all admire.
Take my advice; remain in perfect ease,
Be your teeth black, blue, green, or what you please?

MONRO.

N° 41. SATURDAY, DECEMBER 22, 1787.

He that prefers the boasted excellence of ancient times to the endearments and the embellishments of modern life, may be charged with the depraved taste of the Hottentot, who, on his return to his native country, shook off the European dress, nauseated European food, and indulged in all the excesses of his countrymen.—PARR'S Sermons.

THE declaimers on morals have frequently poured forth their invectives against the living, in favour of the dead. The virtues of past ages have been considered by them as purer than the present, more worthy of imitation, and more conducive to happiness. It will neither be a useless speculation, nor a matter of insuperable difficulty, to explode this vulgar error, and to prove to those who have had the misfortune, as some think it, to be born in the eighteenth century, that it is as free from gross violations of rectitude and decorum as any that have preceded it.

It will be readily admitted by every person of an enlightened understanding, that the number of our public executions can be no criterion of the depravity of our manners, or our progress in vicious refinement. When laws are multiplied to such an immense degree, there must infallibly be more victims to their neglect, as the more cobwebs the spider spins, the more heedless flies are likely to be caught. We leave, therefore, the comparative number of names, which have lately filled the annals of Newgate, to the consideration of the officers of the police, who are most benefited by their augmentation, and who would be most injured, if every statutable offence were not prosecuted to conviction; and proceeding to a review of the religion, the manners, and the amusements of the age, shall draw such conclusions as will abundantly prove our position.

That there is some share of profligacy, infidelity, and irreligion, conspicuously in the present age, few will be hardy enough to deny; but that real virtue, piety, and truth, are both practised and countenanced, must be equally evident, to all whose minds are not tinctured with the gloom of fanaticism, or soured with the leaven of misanthropy. In the church, in the state, in the senate, and at the bar, we have men eminent for the discharge of duty: men who adorn elevated rank by corresponding manners; and are unfashionable enough to think religion has charms, and virtue an inherent lustre.

The present times afford many eminent examples of religion and piety among the highest orders of the state; of the nobility, paying a due respect to the doctrines of Christianity in general, and shewing a promptitude to vindicate the national church in particular; and yet treating dissenters of every denomination with candour and affection. A conduct like this exalts true religion, and points out the alliance of Christianity to Heaven. The prejudices of illiberal minds are always as hostile to its progress, as they are disgraceful to the breast that indulges them. In former days, religion was stained with violence and blood; it now begins to assume its native lustre, and to be marked with its genuine characteristics; it breathes 'peace and good-will to men.'

To form a due estimate of the morals of the present age will be an easy matter. They are influenced by religion; and if the latter be pure and generally practised, the former will of necessity receive a polish from its connexion. That charity triumphs over avarice; that the social obligations are fulfilled with a more exact observance; that the virtues of humanity have gained an ascendancy over cruelty and revenge; are positions that need only be named to be allowed.

It is not to be denied, that former ages were replete with examples of heroism, magnanimity, and a contempt of death: I give them full credit for superior abstemiousness, and more resigned humility: they produced men who were zealous for religion, who were lovers of their country, and foes to tyrants; men, who were valiant in war, and amiable in peace. But where was to be found that polish which is universally diffused over modern manners? that civilization, that mildness, and grace, which repress the bursts of furious passions, and soften the ferocity of rudeness and barbarity?

War, the pest of the human race, and the disgrace of reason, was once carried on with horrors now unknown. The public enemy, when disarmed, is now treated with the indulgence of a private friend; and, instead of dragging the vanquished at our chariot-wheels, humanity and gentleness go hand in hand to soften the severity of defeat, and to reconcile the conquered to himself. The same amiableness of manners is visible in humbler circumstances, and displayed on less important occasions. The snarling cynic may call all this effeminacy, and dignify savage qualities with the appellation of virtues: he may denominate piety a weakness, and stigmatize the humane with want of spirit. But let it be observed, in answer to his cavils, that whatever renders mankind more amiable and more refined, whatever binds one to another with more endearing ties, is a virtue, and a virtue deserving applause.

As manners are intimately connected with our religion, so our amusements have a close affinity to our manners. The boisterous mirth, the rude joy, the indelicate witticism, which used to delight even the highest ranks, are now degraded to the lowest; and if refinement progressively goes on, we may hope in time to see even the lower orders of society too enlightened to taste them. The obstreperous jollity of the bowl, though sometimes admitted, is now no longer boasted of. The most splendid triumphs of Bacchus are not considered as conferring glory on the most zealous of his votaries; and he who can vanquish his companions over the bottle, is as little valued by those who pretend to refinement, as, a few years hence, he will most probably be, who can lay no claims to merit, except his resolution in risking his neck over a five-bar gate; or killing his horse, that he may boast the paltry achievement of being in at the death.

But of all the amusements that modern times can exhibit with just pretensions to applause, the stage, in its present state, is one of the chief. The lewd allusion, the profane jest, and the imprecatory expletives of language, are now relished only by those whose ideas are circumscribed by the meanness of their birth and the scantiness of their education; or whose minds have never imbibed right sentiments of genuine humour and sterling sense. But it is not the public stage to which I would confine my commendations; as its managers have the million to please, they are too often obliged to do violence to their own judgment, in order to gratify a vitiated and vulgar taste. It is the establishment of private theatres that I particularly advert to, as a proof of the superior taste and elegance of this age over every preceding one. This may justly be denominated an era in the scenic art, when trick and artifice are banished, and their places successfully supplied by easy manners. Whoever has had the pleasure of seeing the performances of our nobility and gentry on their own stages, where only the most admired and most decorous pieces are represented, and where the actors appear more ambitious to imitate real life than to shine in affected situations, must confess, that the dominion of taste has widely extended itself, and that frivolous or vicious pastimes are exchanged for rational and instructive pursuits. In consequence of this diffusion of dramatic performances, the stage is more likely than ever to become ' the school of virtue, and the picture of living manners.' For in whatever light the surly dogmatist may consider plays in general, it may be asserted, on safe grounds, that they may be good in particular; they may impart much knowledge without the languor of study, and warn from error without an approach to the verge of guilt. Indeed, where virtue obtains those rewards which Heaven will bestow, and poetic justice should never withhold; and where vice smarts for its crimes, and is not rendered alluring by the attraction of

pleasing qualities; then the stage may be considered as an auxiliary to the pulpit,—for morality and
religion must ever be united.—M.   Mavor.

Nº 42.   SATURDAY, DECEMBER 29, 1787.

Cavendum est, si ipse ædifices, ne extra modum sumtu et
magnificentiâ prodeas.—Cicero.

When Greece and Rome had emerged from barbarism to an exalted state of civilization, a distinguished place among the arts was given to architecture.   The accomplished Pericles, assisted by the
refined genius of Phidias, adorned Athens with those
temples, theatres, and porticos, which even in ruins
have excited the admiration of posterity.   After Au-
gustus had established the peace of the Roman
world, a similar display of magnificence was exhibited; and equalled, or rather surpassed, the glory of
Athens.   This memorable era of architecture is
eminently distinguished by the elegance of the *Pa-
latine Temple of Apollo*, and the sublimity of the
Pantheon.

The progress of refinement from public to private
works must necessarily be private houses, because
nothing is more natural to man than imitation, particularly of that which is the object of his wonder
and applause.   They who daily surveyed such edifices as were remarkable for capaciousness and
grandeur, projected the erection of similar structures upon a more confined plan.   Their designs
were frequently carried to such an excess in the
execution. as to pass the limits of convenience and
economy, and give a loose to the sallies of ostenta-

tion and extravagance. From this source was derived the just indignation with which Demosthenes inveighed against the degenerate Athenians, whose houses eclipsed the public buildings, and were lasting monuments of vanity triumphant over patriotism. The strictures of Horace flow in a similar channel, and plainly indicate that the same preposterous rage for building prevailed among the Romans. Even if we make allowance for the hyperbolical flights of the Lyric Muse, we must still suppose that vast and continued operations of architects were carried on by land and water, ' since a few acres only were left for the exercise of the plough, and the fish were sensible of the contraction of their element.'

The transition from the ancients to the moderns is easy and obvious. It must be confessed, that, like servile copyists, we have too closely followed the originals of our great masters, and have delineated their faults as well as their beauties. The contagion of the building influenza was not peculiar to the Greeks and Romans, but has extended its virulence to this country, where it rages with unabating violence. Neither the acuteness of Pott, nor the erudition of Jebb, are necessary to ascertain its symptoms in various parts of England. Bath, Bristol, Cheltenham, Brighton, and Margate, bear evident marks of its wide diffusion. The metropolis is manifestly the centre of the disease. In other places, the accumulation is made by occasionally adding house to house; but in London, street is suddenly added to street, and square to square. The adjacent villages in a short time undergo a complete transformation, and bear no more resemblance to their original state, than Phyllis the milk-maid does to a lady mayoress. The citizen who, twenty years ago, enjoyed at his country-seat pure air, undisturb-

ed retirement, and an extensive prospect, is now surrounded by a populous neighbourhood. The purity
of the air is sullied with smoke, and the prospect is
cut off by the opposite houses. The retirement is
interrupted by the London cries and the vocifera-
tions of the watchman. In the vicinity of the capital
every situation is propitious to the mason and the
carpenter. Mansions daily arise upon the marshes
of Lambeth, the roads of Kensington, and the hills
of Hampstead. The chain of buildings so closely
unites the country with the town, that the distinction is lost between Cheapside and St. George's-
fields. This idea struck the mind of a child, who
lives at Clapham, with so much force, that he observed, ' if they go on building at such a rate, London will soon be next door to us.'

A strong light is often thrown upon the manners
of a people by their proverbial sayings. When the
Irish are highly enraged, they express a wish which
is not tempered with much of the milk of kindness,
by saying, ' may the spirit of building come upon
you.' If an Irishman be once possessed by this
demon, it is difficult to stop his progress through
bricks and mortar, till he exchanges the superintend-
ence of his workmen for the confinement of a prison.
But this propensity is not merely visible in the environs of Dublin, or upon the shores of Cork; it is
equally a characteristic of the *sister kingdom.*

England can furnish not a few instances of men
of taste who have sold the best oaks of their estates
for gilding and girandoles,—of fathers who have
beggared their families to enjoy the pleasure of seeing green-houses and pineries arise under their inspection,—and of fox-hunters who have begun with
a dog-kennel, and ended with a dwelling-house.
Enough is every day done by the amateurs of Wyat
and Chambers, to palliate the censure of ostentation

and uselessness that is lavishly thrown upon the king's house at Winchester, and the Radcliffe library at Oxford.

My cousin, Obadiah Project, Esq. formerly a respectable deputy of Farringdon Ward Within, retired into the country, when he had reached his grand climacteric, upon a small estate. While he lived in town, his favourite hobby-horse, which was building, had never carried him farther than to change the situation of a door, or erecting a chimney. On settling in his new habitation, as he was no sportsman, he found himself inclined to turn student. His genius led him to peruse books of architecture. For two years nothing pleased him so much as *The Builder's Complete Guide*, *Campbell's Vitruvius*, and *Sandby's Views*. All these heated his imagination with the beauties of palaces, and delighted his eye with the regularity of the orders, for which he felt a vague and confused fondness. He had, perhaps, no more idea of the distinction between a cornice and a colonnade, than the monstrous craws. Unluckily, Sir Maximilian Barleycorn was his neighbour, who had lately erected a house upon the Italian plan. As my cousin was laying out his garden, he found that the soil was composed of a fine vein of clay. It immediately struck him, that bricks might be procured at a very cheap rate. The force of inclination, combined with rivalship, and encouraged by opportunity, is too powerful for man to resist. He, therefore, flew to tell his wife of the grand discovery, and inveighed with much warmth against the smallness of their parlour, the badness of the kitchen floor, and the ruinous state of the garrets. She mildly represented that they had no money to throw away upon a new house, and that the old one might cheaply be put into repair. Her remarks had just as much effect as the advice of the barber and the curate had upon

Don Quixote. The next day he played Geoffrey
Gambado, by taking a ride to consult Mr. Puff, the
architect. Mr. Puff was confident that the old house
must fall down in a day or two, and proposed the
following plan for a new one, which exactly reflected my cousin's ideas. The rooms were to be all
cubes. In front, a Venetian door, with a portico
supported by brick pillars, with wooden capitals;
and six bow-windows. A balcony was proposed,
but afterward given up because it was vulgar. My
cousin retired to a neighbouring cottage. The old
house was pulled down, and the brickmakers began
their operations. Unfortunately the wind happened
to blow in such a direction as to create much annoyance with clouds of smoke from the kilns. Whilst
my cousin was half suffocated and half buried in
rubbish, Sir Maximilian Barleycorn and his lady
came to pay a morning visit. They entered the cottage just at the moment when Mrs. Project was setting the boiler upon the fire, and her husband was
paring potatoes. They were obliged to perform these
offices for themselves, because the only servant for
whom they could find room, had been turned off that
morning for abusing carpenters and masons. Sir
Maximilian hastily took his leave, and swore by his
knighthood, ' that apes were the lowest animals in
the creation.' My cousin had calculated, that as he
burnt his own bricks for home consumption, they
would not be subject to any tax. An exciseman un-
deceived him before the house was finished, by hinting that he had incurred a heavy penalty, which he
was obliged to pay. He contrived, however, to keep
up his spirits, by marking the progress of his house,
and the improvements around it. Not far from the
Venetian door was a horse-pond, which the genius
of Project enlarged into a circular piece of water.
He requested his friends to suggest the most tasty

ornaments. One proposed a shepherd and shepherdess upon a pedestal in the middle: another observed, that if farmer Peascod's gander could be placed in it when company came, they would give him credit for keeping a swan: a third, whose notion of things was improving by frequent visits to Vauxhall, was sure that a tin cascade would look very pretty by moonlight. Project, not liking to take up with one good thing, when four were to be had, resolved to adorn his water with them all. He soon after removed into his new habitation, long before the walls were dry. An ague and fever were the consequence of this rash step. His fever was probably increased by Puff's bill, to pay which he sold the greater part of his estate. During his illness, he gradually awoke to a sense of his late imprudence, requested the forgiveness of his wife for not listening to her advice, and begged me to impress his dying injunctions indelibly on my memory : ' Never build after you are five-and-forty; have five years' income in hand before you lay a brick ; and always calculate the expense at double the estimate.'—Q.

KETT.

Nº 43.   SATURDAY, JANUARY 5, 1788.

Rerum concordia discors.—

SHOULD a Dutchman make his appearance as an opera-dancer, a Frenchman be presented to us as a bruiser, a German as a wit, or a Hottentot as a master of the ceremonies, we should be all ready to exclaim, *they are strangely out of character.* Frequently will this exclamation proceed from any one who is attentive to the language which flows around him, as he passes through the crowded streets of London. He will observe, not without some surprise, the bold and venturesome bargains of a mean and squalid-looking miser; he will hear the declamatory discussions of a political peruke-maker, and be disgusted with the technical vulgarities of a jocky lord. Let him transfer his attention from the conversation to the lives and conduct of mankind, and a short series of events will teach him not to be surprised, should he find inconsistencies as unaccountable, and as motley a mixture of heterogeneous qualities. Chance may discover to him situations wherein the fop becomes a sloven, the rebel a tyrant, the sycophant a churl, the patriot a courtier, and the libertine a religious disputant. He who is hackneyed in the ways of men is gradually familiarized to these incongruities. The frequent occurrence of what might at first amaze him, loses the power of exciting surprise when it loses its novelty. That which was formerly beheld with astonishment and aversion is at length regarded with fixed unconcern, or calm acquiescence.

The storms of the ocean were once terrible to the boy, who, now he is become a mariner, surveys them without dread, and hears them without complaint.

The incongruities above-mentioned do not confine themselves to particular characters, but are so universally diffused through all ranks and denominations of men, as to appear not so much the mark of particular failings, as a general characteristic of our nature, a common ingredient in the human constitution, from the flippant levities of the boy too tall for school, to the serious and solemn trifling of the philosopher. Who has not observed the moralist deal forth his lessons of virtue to the world, while he declares by his conduct that he doubts the efficacy of his own doctrine? He extols the value of time, while he suffers it to pass in idle complaints or fruitless contemplation on the rapidity of its flight. He can ascertain, with nice accurate distinctions, the boundaries of virtue and vice; he can exhort us to the practice of the former with the volubility of declamation, or deter us from the latter by exposing it with the poignancy of animated ridicule. But it too frequently happens, that Cicero with the public is Clodius at home, and that in the armour of the Christian hero we find Sir Richard Steele. All the palliations which friendship could suggest to the biographer of Savage have not been able to hide from the world the imprudence, the folly, and the vice, for which he might be stigmatized, from his own writings.

Quam temere in nosmet legem sancimus iniquam.

It is, perhaps, necessary, that for the duration of one good disposition of mind, another should exist by way of relief to it. Vivacity is a proper companion for Seriousnsss, Cheerfulness for Piety, and Condescension for Magnanimity.

——Alterius sic
Altera poscit opem res, et conjurat amice.

Such a contrast has a fine effect in the picture of the soul. It is a virtue in him who holds the most elevated situation occasionally to lay aside the formalities of his rank without degrading himself; for greatness, even if regal, must have its relaxations. The bow which is always bent loses much of its elasticity. The wisdom and exalted character of Agesilaus did not present him from engaging in puerile amusements with his children. The virtuous Scipio and the sagacious Lælius diverted themselves with picking up shells upon the sea-shore. To draw an example from more recent times, the great Newton not unfrequently left the causes of the tides, and the eccentricities of comets, to play with his cat.

Such is the motley tablet of man's mind, that we see painted upon it not only the mixed colours of virtue and vice, but of virtues which assist, and of vices which increase, by supporting each other. Generosity disciplined by prudence makes its possessor liberal without profusion, and an economist without parsimony. It preserves him from the imputation of weakness by misplaced benevolence, and thereby furnishes him with the double power of holding out assistance to those who want it.

Although the mists of prejudice had gathered thick around Johnson when he became the biographer of Swift, he could not but vindicate his parsimony from the censure of meanness, because it was exercised only as the auxiliary to his beneficence. Generosity, indeed, may be considered as the projectile force of the mind, which would fly off to the most extravagant length, did not prudence act as a power of attraction to keep it within its proper orbit.

The same bosom is oftentimes distracted by the conflict of contending passions, totally different in their exertions, but alike baneful in their influence. Prodigality and avarice meet but to try whether the one can scatter with the wilder extravagance, or the other save with the more rigorous and unwearied meanness. Thus are they alternately encouraged by each other. Avarice furnishes the means for profusion, and profusion makes avarice more necessary. ' To be greedy of the property of others, and lavish of his own,' were the strongest traits of Catiline's mind. In modern life, among those who are cursed with a similar disposition, no one is more remarkable than the *gamester*.

Cruelty and cowardice, ignorance and presumption, insolence and servility, are the general associates, yet the general opponents. They are united to harass each other; they engage, and, like Antæus, gather strength from every defeat. He who can contemplate these inconsistencies, and attempt to reconcile such absurdities to reason, may hunt for beauties in Ossian, or unalloyed purity in a Birmingham coin; or should he find such toil ineffectual, let him extract candour from a professed critic, ransack the world for an attorney of moderate peculation and tolerable honesty, or listen with credulity to the narrative of Captain Lemuel Gulliver.

How frequent are our exclamations, in a shameful spirit of studied negligence, or listless inactivity, that time is a heavy burden to us! how loud are our complaints that we have nothing to do! Yet how inconsistent are these exclamations, and these complaints, with the declarations which truth and reason so often extort from us, that the flight of time reproaches us with our supineness, and that a day never passes without our ' having left undone those things which we ought to have done!'

While we are thus capricious and contradictory in our actions and opinions, ever wishing that completed which we ever delay to begin, lamenting over imaginary wants, neglecting to enjoy blessings we possess, grasping at the fleeting phantom of happiness, and regardless of the substantial form of it, human life appears like a patchwork of ill-sorted colours; like the fantastic and incongruous phantasms of a dream, or, for aught I know, like the miscellaneous ingredients of an Olla Podrida.

MONRO.

N° 44   SATURDAY, JANUARY 12, 1787.

A te principium, tibi desinet.—VIRG.

Of self so dear I sang in number one,
By self so dear I'll end as I've begun.

IF there be any of my readers, whether inhabiting
the retirements of the Isle of Muck, frequenters of
the religious receptacles of St. James's or St. Giles's,
or tenants of a bow-window in Shoe-lane, to whom
it shall be a matter of momentary concern that they
are now reading the last number of the Olla Podrida;
to such I would return thanks for the patience with
which they have toiled through my pages, and administer some consolation under their present disappointment. I have the satisfaction to reflect, that
I take my leave of the world at a time when it cannot be at a loss for amusement. The of Isle Muck
has, no doubt, those pleasing recreations by which
the gloom of a winter's evening is easily dissipated.
The exercise of hot-cockles, and the agreeable diversion of blindman's-buff, has most likely found its
way even to the inmost of the Hebrides, where simplicity has so firmly withstood the inroads of refinement, and where a deviation from barbarism seems
to have been considered as a defection from virtue.
Let me remind my friends in Shoe-lane likewise,
that the cessation of this paper's appearance amongst
them ought not to be considered as a calamity, while
the season furnishes such a variety of entertainment:
he who, from reasons which I will not pretend to inquire into, has perused with any degree of pleasure
the numbers of this work, now finds his mental
amusement happily diversified by ' The Bellman's
Address to his Masters and Mistresses all;' in which,
I must add, be he poet, moralist, philosopher, or

lounger, he will meet with ample subject for discussion or contemplation.

Amongst other traits of our national character, I know not that our observance of religious festivals has ever been noticed. The histories of nations furnish us with no examples of such annual enthusiasm as marks the inhabitants of Great Britain. Christmas never visits us without a train of peculiar rites and ceremonies, to which I suppose our historians have not extended their notice, because they have been unwilling to deal forth their censures upon their countrymen. How we ought to commemorate this season, every one may know ; how we do commemorate it, no one is ignorant ; and there is perhaps not much distinction between the omissions of him who neglects to practise what he knows is right, and of him who is ignorant of what he ought to know. But as it is considerably to my interest to bid farewell to my readers, without leaving them in ill-humour, I shall lay a restraint upon my inclination to moralize, and be very brief upon a subject which perhaps demands a more ample discussion. To the serious it is unnecessary to suggest, that the time is now present which they are called upon, by their reason and their religion, to welcome with every demonstration of rational and settled joy. These are reflections to which they are naturally led without exhortation, and which the gay might indulge without diminution of their happiness. Yet some there are, who, without taste for the enjoyment of gaiety, are never disposed to seriousness ; who, from a trifling disposition, are devoted to endless insipidity, and affected mirth ; or, from vicious tendencies, are willing to banish reflection, lest it should bring with it an interruption to their supposed happiness. But lest I should seem already to have forgotten my promise of restraining my inclination to moralize, I shall fill up part of my va-

cant page with that beautiful sonnet of Shakspeare,
so well describing the natural appearance of winter.
If there be any one to whom it is new, I shall be
entitled to his thanks; and he, to whom it is familiar, cannot read it again without pleasure. Its
simplicity I know not how sufficiently to commend.

> When icicles hang by the wall,
>   And Dick the shepherd blows his nail
> And Tom bears logs into the hall,
>   And milk comes frozen home in pail:
> When blood is nipt, and ways be foul;
> Then nightly sings the staring owl
> Tu-whit, tu-whoo, a merry note,
> While greasy Joan doth keel the pot.
>
> When all around the wind doth blow,
>   And coughing drowns the parson's saw,
> And birds sit brooding in the snow,
>   And Marian's nose looks red and raw,
> When roasted crabs hiss in the bowl;
> Then nightly sings the staring owl
> Tu-whit, tu-whoo, a merry note,
> While greasy Joan doth keel the pot.

With regard to the tendency of these pages which
I here offer to the public, I know my own intentions and am satisfied. How they are executed, it
remains for them to judge. To the critics I have
nothing to say. He who would shun criticism must
not be a scribbler; and he who would court it must
have great abilities or great folly.

MONRO.

END OF VOL. XLI.

Printed by J. F. Dove, St. John's Square.

... that beautiful sonnet of Shakspeare,
... describing the natural appearance of winter.
If there are any due to whom it is due, I shall be
... to his thanks; and he, to whom it is must,
... capable read it again without pleasure. But
... simplicity I know not how sufficiently to commend

When icicles hang by the wall,
And Dick the shepherd blows his nail,
And Tom bears logs into the hall,
And milk comes frozen home in pail,
When blood is nipt and ways be foul,
Then nightly sings the staring owl,
Tu-whit, tu-who, a merry note,
While greasy Joan doth keel the pot.

When all aloud the wind doth blow,
And coughing drowns the parson's saw,
And birds sit brooding in the snow,
And Marian's nose looks red and raw,
When roasted crabs hiss in the bowl,
Then nightly sings the staring owl,
Tu-whit, tu-who, a merry note,
While greasy Joan doth keel the pot.

With regard to the tendency of these pages which
I here offer to the public, I know my own intentions and am satisfied. How they are executed, it
remains for them to judge. To the critic I have
nothing to say. He who would shun criticism must
not be a scribbler; and he who could court it must
have great abilities or great vanity.

MOORE.